MW01292478

Lick and Turn

Savoring Every Drop of
God's Goodness

A Memoir of Dave & Jen Bell

Written by Terry Gray

This book is a memoir, written from the oral recollections of Dave and Jen Bell and the events of their lives. As such, it is based on memory and perspective. Every effort has been made to portray the story as accurately as possible, and facts that could be verified through reliable sources were. All stories are true, although some names and details have been omitted or changed to respect the privacy of those involved.

Cover design by Jarob Bramlett

Dedicated with love to those who went before us
to cheer us on from Heaven:
Patricia Baker, Bud House,
Jennie Bell, and Mariellen Miller.
Your love and never-failing support is sorely missed.
We love you and cannot wait to celebrate
with you again one day.

And to all the precious children
created by God who were abandoned.
God makes no mistakes.
You are loved!

Contents

Author's Acknowledgments

To God be the glory!

Completing my first book, *Unsinkable*, was what I thought at the time a once-in-a-lifetime accomplishment. No one was more surprised than me when I began to feel the need to write again, to help others share their stories of God's workings in their lives. When Dave and Jen Bell, childhood friends of mine, asked if I might consider helping them tell their story of God's goodness, I was honored that they would choose me to facilitate such an important task and jumped at the opportunity.

Even though I never doubted God's calling to write this book, my timing was, as usual, different than His. Just as I began eagerly writing in early spring 2015, life blind-sided me with some terrible, devastating blows. My dear sweet Dad, who had been steadily fighting a losing battle with Alzheimer's for a couple of years, suffered an unexpectedly sudden downward spiral in his deteriorating health. Due to what we believe were two strokes, he fell and hit his head twice in one day, banging himself up badly and causing a brain bleed that ultimately took his life. My last coherent visit with Daddy was the morning after his first fall, holding his hand and looking through my own teary eyes into his bruised and battered face, telling him how sorry I was that he had to go through this. In a rare moment of clarity, he looked straight at me with his crystal clear blue eyes and spoke words I will always treasure. "God has a plan. We don't always know what it is or understand it, but He has a plan. We have to trust Him."

One month later, Daddy went to Heaven. That same day I had my first chemotherapy treatment for stage 3 rectal cancer.

Daddy never knew I had cancer. The diagnosis was shocking, coming the day before my 58th birthday and just eight days after my last conversation with him. He never knew how much strength those words would give me in the months to come…weeks and weeks of chemo, radiation, two major surgeries with a temporary ileostomy in between. Every day was a struggle, and this book was necessarily and indefinitely put on hold.

Through those dark days, God was there every step of the way. I knew it, I felt it in the heart of my very being. As painful and difficult as those 15 months were, God used that season to refine and grow me, and although it obviously wasn't a journey I would have chosen, I am not sorry to have taken it.

God's timing is not ours. So nearly two years after I set this manuscript aside, I picked it up again and began writing. As it turns out, the book's completion comes at a natural break in the ministry lives of Dave and Jen, coinciding with the completion of the building of the new Mahali pa Maisha infant rescue center campus. God's timing, not ours.

There are no words to convey the love and appreciation I have for my husband Kim, who has always supported me in whatever endeavor and challenge God has thrown my way. He is the wisest person I know, my best friend and the love of my life, and my number one fan, and I thank God every day for blessing me with such a precious man with which to share my life.

Thanks also to my four terrific children, Kristoffer, Emily, Kamaron, and Kyler, as well as their wonderful spouses. I often feel so unworthy of your unconditional love and support, but I am so very grateful to be your mom! And to my eight grandchildren…Karter,

Kaden, Kassie, Kelsey, Krew, Juni, Abram, and Lucy... remember that Gramaw and Jesus will always love you no matter what!

At 81 years young, Mama continues to inspire me! I can only hope to be half the woman of God that she is "when I grow up." She was my first love and I owe more to her than I could ever repay. And even now not a day passes without me smiling in fond remembrance of Dad. His final words to me will forever be etched on my heart!

A special shout-out of gratitude to my brother-in-law Kent, who graciously gave up some of his precious summer hours editing these words and helping be sure my sometimes-rambling thoughts made sense. He is a wonderful person and another wise Gray man.

So many friends and extended family make my life full and complete...I am so very thankful to each of them for their love and support. I dare not try naming them, but each of you holds a very treasured place in my life. Thank you for putting up with me!

To my dear friends, Dave and Jen, I thank you for entrusting the telling of your story to me. I so appreciate the detailed newsletters you painstakingly wrote and kept over the years, which helped tremendously in the writing. It's been an incredible privilege to share in even such a small way God's amazing working in your life. You inspire me daily with your unselfish servants' hearts.

But above all, I give all praise and honor to God for walking beside me on this journey this side of Eternity. To Him be the glory!

Terry Gray, July 2017

The Bells' Acknowledgments

"Trust in the Lord with all your heart, then lick and turn!"

The creation of this book came about as almost a joke. We thoroughly enjoyed reading Terry's first book, *Unsinkable*, about a friend we grew up knowing. So we halfheartedly mentioned she should write our story, never imagining that it might actually happen! Terry has been a true Godsend for us personally, and for the ministry of Mahali pa Maisha. Who would have thought all those years ago when that bratty Bell kid was picking on that older girl as they rode the school bus, well, that is another story…

We are extremely grateful for Terry's tenacity as she battled personal battles of her own during the creation of this book. Above all, we are grateful for her hunger, desire, and stamina in her relentless pursuit of Jesus and how He called her to serve this ministry.

The journey from there to here has been filled with some crazy roller-coaster moments. Not only for us (Dave and Jen), but also for the many who stepped or were thrust into our lives.

We often joke about God's Fingerprints on our lives, we can now see them as we look backwards in time. And spending time with Terry writing this book certainly brought even more of those "God moments" back to life in our memories. Many events of our lives could not have been orchestrated by any other means than our Father in Heaven.

Even during the actual writing of the book, God stepped in and said "Wait," time and time again. So many things were happening in the ministry and in our personal lives that it was clear God knew we, and Terry as well, needed some time. And we learned to be okay with that, it was God's time.

Our lives have involved a lot of sacrifice. Sadly it was mostly sacrifices made by others. Our sons Chris and Nate gave up a lot as we pulled them out of a life of "normal." Nothing quite disrupts friendships and relationships like traveling all over the world. They made countless sacrifices as they gave up many of their "toys", playing baseball, and perhaps most of all a place to call "Home" that did not change on a regular schedule. In spite of the way we "messed up" your lives, you have always supported us and we could not have asked for better kids to travel much of this journey with us. We love you.

Later it was sacrifices made by our daughter-in-law Ariel and our two precious grandsons, Miles and Paxton. Nothing says "I love you" like time. And we know that our time with you is preciously small. One of the most difficult things about serving around the world is missing family…parties and picnics, ball games, and so much more. We know it gets confusing when Grandma and Grandpa fly into your lives for a few weeks a year, and seem to try to spend every waking moment with you. Please know if it was possible we would be with you EVERY moment we are home! Facebook updates help, but it is so hard to watch you grow up from 8000 miles away.

To our parents, Earl and Patricia Baker, and Myron and Phyllis Bell. If this book did nothing else it walked us back through the realization of how much of a debt we owe you for all the years and tears you poured into our lives. Any of the "good" that may have come from our footsteps and God-chosen journey can be directly attributed to you. For all the wandering from the right path, well, we take full responsibility for that. We love you and pray that we can achieve even a small impact on others like you had on us.

We started to name the many friends, who are much more like family, but this acknowledgment would be several pages long. Suffice it to say, those who were a big part of our "growing" years know who you are. So many opened their homes and lives to us, especially during the time of selling out and living like vagabonds as we tried to find just where God would have us serve.

There are so many individuals that have impacted our walk and made this journey possible. From the many partners, both individuals and churches, who gave sacrificially during the campaign to develop the Mahali pa Maisha property, to those what have consistently been faithful team members and made the day-to-day operations possible. It takes an army of Baby Boosters to provide the diapers, formula, medical care, and so much more. So from the bottom of our hearts, we want to thank you.

We also owe a debt of gratitude to our Kenyan staff. You are our family away from our family. Many of you have been with us most of our Kenyan life. It has truly been an honor to serve alongside you.

Each step of this journey we felt and saw God's presence and fingerprints. We are eternally grateful to our Lord Jesus Christ for allowing us this honor of being His hands and feet for the little ones.

Dave and Jen Bell, July 2017

"Trust in the Lord with all your heart and
lean not on your own understanding;
in all your ways acknowledge Him,
and He will make your paths straight."

Proverbs 3: 5-6

Maps

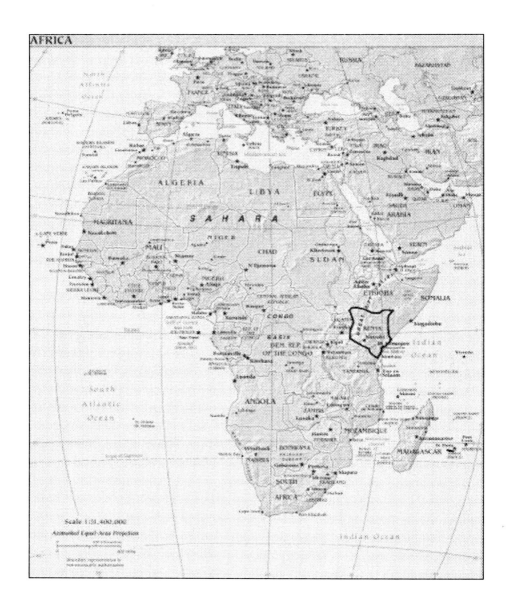

Public domain maps (CIA) from Wikimedia Commons

Prologue

A warm day, June 2000

Hagerstown, Indiana USA

The hot mid-day sun beat down on Dave's head as he re-tightened the straps across the bed of his pick-up truck. This was it, the day for which he'd planned and anxiously anticipated for weeks. His heart was beating a little faster than normal, either from exertion or excitement. It was hard to tell which. Probably a combination of both.

Dave walked around the truck and tested the straps on the other side. Everything seemed to be secure. They weren't going far, he told himself.

But no, that wasn't true at all. In actuality, they were going very far...far, far away from family and all that was familiar, very far away from this life he had known all his 40 years on this earth and the life he and Jen had shared together for 18 years now. Yes, they were going far away. The craziest thing of all was, Dave had no idea of their destination.

Opening the driver's door, Dave paused for one last look. Off to his left was the lovely gray farmhouse, shaded by mature trees. He and Jen had worked so hard to fix it up, remodeling and redecorating it into their dream home. So many wonderful memories they had made there! Out in the yard, the boys' play set. How many hours had he spent playing with them here, soaking up their laughter at the only home they had ever known? Dave looked further behind him, beyond the house and yard to the tool shop, the shop he had started a few years ago and had successfully built into a profitable business.

The American dream. Dave had it. A beautiful wife and two great sons, a nice home, and a thriving business he'd built from scratch. He had it all! A man's dream-come-true, more than he'd ever hoped for and certainly more than he deserved.

One last glance through misted eyes, Dave climbed into the truck cab. In the seat behind him, Chris and Nate, ages 16 and 10, were unusually quiet and deep in their own thoughts. Jen quietly smiled reassuringly as he slid beneath the steering wheel. There was no need for words between them now; there'd been plenty of words in the past several weeks, yes, even months before.

Dave started the truck and looked up into the rearview mirror. Everything they owned was tucked beneath those straps in the truck bed…a few pieces of family heirloom furniture that Jen had inherited from her grandparents, keepsake boxes of the boys' baby pictures and memorabilia, a hope chest Dave had given to Jen years ago, dishes and some basic kitchen supplies, and a couple of suitcases of clothing. All their worldly belongings, everything they owned, packed into the back of that black and silver Dodge Ram.

He didn't look back, but instead turned his head toward his lovely bride and smiled. At that moment, pulling out onto State Road 38 and away from everything he'd ever known, Dave felt happier and freer than he'd ever felt in his entire life.

CHAPTER 1

Country Boy

July, late 1960s

Bell Family Farm outside of Mooreland, Indiana

Loose wisps of copper hair tickled her cheeks as she gently pulled the dancing curtains aside. What a blessing was that breeze, making the oppressive Indiana summer heat at least tolerable. Rippling across the ripening fields, over the mown lawn, and through the kitchen's screened windows, the warm wafts caused the muslin curtains to sway in delight and her lips to curve into a smile.

Phyllis couldn't help smiling as she gazed out her kitchen windows, quickly scanning the grassy yard outside. She never tired of this view, her own little piece of paradise. Her bright eyes, long-practiced at spotting and counting, moved from the barn across the backyard and out toward the fields and woods beyond. Faint sounds of children's voices and laughter mixed with the singing of birds and the distant lowing of cows and the steady hum of a lawn mower, a symphony of sounds that was pure musical delight to her ears. Yes, she loved this little spot in the middle of Indiana farm country, so very near to where she and her husband Myron had grown up themselves.

She could hear the little sisters playing, Jeanna and Mariellen entertaining and watching her youngest, Trecia. Their giggling and chatter told Phyllis all she needed to know, that they were safe and sound and happy, probably playing with the newest batch of barn kittens that they'd come to love. How those kittens ever put up with so many eager and not-so-gentle hands, Phyllis would never understand.

Just beyond the barn, Phyllis saw Ross dutifully making his rounds on the mower. He'd stripped off his shirt in the summer heat, a boy on the cusp of manhood lately thinking himself more adult than he really was. Phyllis smiled, a hint of sadness that her brood was growing up so very quickly right before her eyes.

Juli, her oldest daughter, was busy inside the farmhouse behind her. A teenager now, Juli didn't often have time for barn kitties and such, although she secretly vacillated between wanting to be grown-up and still be a little girl. Chuck and Rex, her two oldest, were nearly men already. How was it possible that Chuck was already out of high school and Rex getting ready to start his senior year?! As was often the case these days, they weren't home but instead working to earn money for their inevitable date plans for the coming weekend.

God had abundantly blessed the marriage of Phyllis and her beloved husband Myron. The two of them had met as teenagers at a Friday night party at the home of one of Phyllis's girlfriends. Phyllis secretly had a shine for Richard, one of the boys at the party, and when Richard was injured horsing around in the yard, Myron, being the only one with a car, drove them all to the hospital. It was while they were waiting for Richard to be treated that Myron and Phyllis became friends. Soon after, Myron used his car as leverage to get a real first "date" with his new friend Phyllis, and after that double-date with their friends, Richard fell off her radar. Phyllis knew she'd found the man she was looking for and it was all Myron from that day forward.

But after Phyllis headed to college that fall, the romance floundered. Myron would drive up to see her every few weeks, but it was too long between visits and Phyllis decided it was probably best for them to break it off for a while. When she came home from college that spring and was working at the tiny small-town bank, Phyllis fell head-over-heels for Myron all over again. When she'd look out the bank windows and see him strolling by, she couldn't help but regret her decision and wonder why she'd ever let him go. When Myron called her later that summer, Phyllis decided she wasn't going to let him go again.

And she didn't. In September of 1948, the two of them were married. While they had hoped to be married in the White Branch Church of the Brethren, the charming country church in which Phyllis had grown up, it was undergoing renovations at the time, so Phyllis and Myron exchanged their vows in the home where Phyllis was reared.

Soon the children began to come. Eight children, eight perfect miracles, all gifts from God! Over the years, friends and family had questioned them often about the wisdom and size of their continually-growing family. But to Phyllis and Myron, each baby that came along was another precious blessing, a gift that thrilled them. Phyllis had always said she wouldn't get married until she found someone who wanted six children. Myron said he'd always thought seven would be nice. And over a span of 15 years, God had blessed them with eight.

Peering out the kitchen window that sunny July day, her mind automatically clicked them off, one by one, as Phyllis accounted for her children. She knew where seven of them were, but where was David? That boy! He was the real reason Phyllis had to do so much checking on her children. There was never any knowing what David would be up to.

David was number seven of eight, and he had been a handful from the day he took his first breath. Born September 12, 1960, he made himself known from the very beginning. David may have been part of a large family, but he was not going to get lost in the crowd. Many a time his twinkling eyes and cute dimples had saved his hide from spankings he surely deserved. David was a spark, and no matter how much exasperation he sometimes caused Phyllis and Myron, his charming ways always made her heart smile.

Just like it was smiling now. Phyllis spotted her tow-headed rascal of a boy rounding the edge of the barn just as she was thinking she needed to head out to find him. There he was, astride that crazy big old goat San Fernando Red. Riding that goat, pretending he's a cowboy. Yep, that was her David!

How or why that goat got its name, no one ever really knew. But he was a family pet, with no fences or pens to hold him in. San Fernando roamed the farmhouse yard just like one of the many dogs or cats or other pets that the family had over the years. David had even ridden San Fernando in the local Mooreland Fair Pet Parade, a huge and much-anticipated summer event in their small farm community. The goat was ornery and stubborn, but seemed to have met his match with young David, and those two mischievous boys seemed to have a special bond. Add to the mix the 14-year-old turkey Matilda who often followed Red and David around, an unlikely threesome to be sure.

Phyllis drew her head away from the billowing curtains and back into the kitchen, her motherly instincts temporarily appeased as she went back to her ever-constant meal preparations. Dinner was a special family time and, as much work as it was, Phyllis enjoyed turning her garden-grown vegetables and home-grown beef into delicious meals for her hungry family. Soon they whole gang would be clamoring for supper, and she best get busy making it.

David Bell, 6 years old 1966

A few years later, on a cold February morning

Same farmhouse

Rap, rap, RAP! David tumbled over in bed, his foggy mind hoping beyond hope that he was just having a dream. The comfy quilt entangled his legs, so warm and cozy against the bitter wind that had howled and lulled him to sleep the night before. Somewhere halfway between slumber and wakefulness, he heard it again. This time it was unmistakable.

Rap, RAP, **RAP!!!**

He didn't need a clock to tell him it was very early in the morning, hours before the sun would even show its bright face across the frosty fields. Unwillingly but out of long-established habit, David shook his groggy head and threw his legs over the side of the bed, out of their toasty bedclothes and into the cold, dark room. Eyes barely open, he tugged on his jeans, sweatshirt, and socks and made his way along the dark upstairs hallway and down the steps.

The cows didn't know or care that it was too early and too dark and too cold for a boy like David. All they knew was that their udders were full and it was milking time. And that rapping? Myron was ready for the boys to help with the pre-dawn milking chores. When Dad knocked that second time, David and the others knew they better get moving or else. Even though he'd been helping Dad with the milking chores since he could barely walk, getting out of his warm bed before daylight never got any easier.

David tugged on his barn clothes and opened the door. The frigid air, no longer howling but now still and quiet, smacked him awake. He walked toward the lighted windows of the milk barn, knowing the cows and Dad awaited him, neither of them particularly patiently.

Opening the door, the ever-so-familiar smells of cattle assailed his senses. Many people thought cows stunk, but David wasn't really so sure about that. The smells and sounds of the gentle animals were as much a part of him as the farmland where he worked and played, the cows part of his small secure world. On mornings like this, they seemed to be hovering in a misty fog as their breathing condensed around their warm bodies inside the small milking chambers. The cows were more like family members than they were livestock, and David knew the personalities and quirks of each one.

With over 50 cows to milk and only ten milking stanchions, it took more than an hour for the twice-daily chore to be completed. While his older brothers helped Myron handle the cows and put the milkers on their swollen teats, it was David's job to help get them into the stanchions and settled down. Using feed to entice them, he'd go along the row and pour the grain into the troughs, talking to the cows along the way. When David had the ten cows happily munching their breakfasts while Dad and his brothers were milking them, he'd often lay down on top of the feed sacks and catch a quick snooze before it was time for the next batch of cows to be brought inside. If he timed it perfectly, he could get another hour of sleep in before heading off to school.

David and his family knew the routine inside and out. While Myron and the boys were in the barn, Phyllis was in the kitchen preparing breakfast and the girls were getting in and out of the farmhouse's only bathroom, readying themselves for school so they'd be out of the way when the boys were finished. Most days the system worked well, but there wasn't much extra time for error. The children could not afford to miss the school bus, as their wide age spread caused them to be scattered amongst several small schools in the community and the last thing Myron wanted to do was to run them from one end of the county to the other to get them to their different schools.

Late afternoons, when Myron got home after working a regular shift at his factory job, it would be time to milk again. Twice a day, every day, for as long as David could remember. Oftentimes, the cows were reluctant to leave their pastures and even hollering "Sic cow, sic cow" wouldn't get them headed toward the barn fast enough. Cowboy David would hop on Red, or sometimes a Hereford bull named Clyde, and round up the cows out of the pasture and urge them toward the milkhouse.

The obligation of twice-daily milking kept the family close to home nearly all the time. But occasionally they'd get someone to take care of the milking chores so they could take a family vacation, like the very memorable time when the Bell clan drove down to Disney World. David still treasured that sombrero that he had bought with his very own money that trip. But family vacations didn't happen often. Money was tight, and traveling with such a large troupe was not an easy undertaking.

Despite the ten years of age difference that separated them, David held a special fondness for his oldest brother Chuck. Being ten years his senior, Chuck was like a second father to young David, showing much patience when his little brother tagged along on his hunting and trapping trips. He and David shared a love of everything outdoors, and David saw a hero when he looked at his big brother. When Chuck left for Manchester College, David was lost and oftentimes felt like he'd lost his best friend. David begged to tag along when Chuck came home for the weekend and headed out to trap rodents for college biology class, and Chuck endured David's "help" many times while honing his photography skills. David adored Chuck, and for years later a curled photograph of a turtle that Chuck had given him still graced David's bulletin board, a reminder of the big brother he wanted to be "just like" when he grew up.

During the school year free hours were few, but during the summers...oh my! Summers were glorious on the farm. While the chores didn't stop but instead actually increased during the summer, there were also many free hours for exploring and playing. David loved to spend time in the woods as well as fishing in the creek. With his many siblings and pets, David was never at a loss for playmates, but often he just enjoyed being by himself in the woods, imagining himself an adventurer and hunting with his stick gun the pretend wild African animals that roamed their Indiana woods. An old abandoned car, that had been there longer than his family, made a great clubhouse or rocket ship or whatever he imagined it to be.

Even the big white barn was a dream playhouse for a country boy. David and Mariellen, who was just two years older than he, loved being daredevils and walking the boards of the hay mow, a dangerous activity that had Phyllis been aware of would surely not have been allowed. But most of the time, David avoided injuries, at least something serious enough to warrant medical attention.

There was the time that he rode Ross's minibike down the hill, losing control and running smack-dab into the corner of the milkhouse. Fortunately, Ross was nearby and carried him to the house, his fear over his unconscious brother momentarily out-weighing his anger about the damaged minibike. Phyllis and Myron loaded David in the station wagon and took him to the hospital. David's week-long stay in the facility cost him a chance to win the sixth-grade chess tourney and also caused him to miss the family Easter celebrations and the sweet treats he always enjoyed from the traditional egg hunt that day. For once in David's life, his siblings felt sorry for him and thrilled him with a bounty of candy while David was still unhappily confined to his hospital bed.

One other time, David had fallen while chasing his sisters and had dislocated his thumb, which to him wasn't all that serious as he vehemently insisted he did not need to go to the doctor because "I can still eat." As long as David could eat, life was good.

Yes, David did love to eat. There were times Phyllis wondered if she'd ever be able to fill her boy up! Fortunately, there was always plenty of food in the larder and fresh eggs and milk every day to keep her large family fed. The children weren't thrilled about helping in the garden, but they sure enjoyed the fruits of their labors when they later appeared on the dinner table.

Although dinners out with their family of ten didn't happen often, it was a treat when Myron and Phyllis would load everyone up for a restaurant meal. Encouraged by his parents to order water for his beverage, David always insisted that water just didn't quench his thirst and wanted to order the rare treat of a soda instead. And once, when the waitress at Cattlemen's Restaurant brought out a huge platter of fried chicken for their family-style meal, David's face broke out in a huge grin and he smacked his lips at the sight. "Looks like we came to the right place this time!" Yes, David always loved a good meal.

Every so often, to celebrate a special occasion or just for fun, Myron and Phyllis would treat their family with a trip to Miller's Ice Cream in nearby Cambridge City. Each one would get an ice cream cone with wise instructions from Dad to keep the ice cream under control, "Lick and turn. Lick and turn." David found it hard to keep his tongue ahead of the melting treat, but he sure didn't want to miss one single sweet drop!

Not every ice cream outing turned out quite as planned. One memorable trip when the Bells decided an ice cream treat was the perfect way to celebrate the purchase of a new family station wagon, David promptly christened the pristine vehicle by spilling his entire chocolate milkshake down one of the rear speakers. Although the family would laugh about it later, there was certainly no laughing that day as David received yet another deserved spanking.

Summers also meant 4-H was in full swing, with the Henry County Fair a July highlight every year. Like most country kids and following in his siblings' footsteps, David was active in 4-H and especially enjoyed showing cows he had raised on their farm. Over the years, David raised several calves and was especially proud of Allison Golden Wonderful Bell, he and Goldie winning the Grand Champion trophy two years in a row. Of course, 4-H calves are usually auctioned off at the end of the fair, and David was a bit traumatized when not long after his calf dubbed "Arby" was sold, the family passed an Arby's restaurant in a nearby city and David suddenly and uncharacteristically lost his appetite.

Much of the Bells' family life revolved around church. Myron and Phyllis both had a deep love for Jesus and a strong Christian faith, and they reared their children to embrace those beliefs as well. White Branch Church of the Brethren, a small country congregation just a few miles down the road, was like a second home to David and the folks there like his second family. Phyllis had grown up in that church, and she and Myron faithfully took their brood to Sunday School and worship every week. Sundays were church days, followed by a big family dinner and a free afternoon with his family and often his cousins. David enjoyed the freedom of Sundays and looked forward to the special family day. While he was still too young to realize all the implications of dedicating his life to Christ, at eleven years old David, along with a few of his friends, was baptized by long-time pastor Leonard Lutz on a hot summer Sunday morning, dunked under the waters of the White Branch Church baptistry that was tucked behind the long, burgundy velvet curtains that hung in the front of the small sanctuary.

David always spent a week of his summer at Camp Mack in northern Indiana, the same church camp where his mother had gone as a little girl, as well as each one of his brothers and sisters before him. David looked forward to church camp every year and made many memories there on the banks of Lake Waubee. It was at Camp Mack that David and his sister Mariellen made a pact with each other that they would never smoke or do drugs. Church camp was one of every summer's highlights, and not primarily because of the spiritual growth involved. While there were of course daily devotions and Bible lessons and lots of talking about Jesus, the real lure of Camp Mack was that it was a week away from the farm chores and the watchful eyes of Mom and Dad, a time to have fun!

But try as he might, an ornery boy like David wasn't always able to steer away from childhood trouble. Trouble seemed to find him, nothing really serious in the big scheme of life, but he did earn many a spanking along the way. Climbing the apple tree by the road and throwing apples at passing cars just did not amuse the drivers as much as it did David. Momma Phyllis was not happy when one day she sent David to collect the eggs and he came back empty-handed, for some unknown reason deciding to throw the eggs against the chicken house and breaking every single one. And one day for the same unknown reasons, David decided to practice his baseball batting skills by knocking out the long line of windows on the chicken house. Sometimes the boy just couldn't seem to control himself, even if it did mean yet another spanking from Dad.

Howard, a local man who drove the Bell children's school bus, may or may not have stopped by the Bell house a time or two to discuss David's bus behavior with Phyllis and Myron. His parents always took care of the situation, and David learned his lessons the hard way at times. Then there was the time that David decided to climb up his mother's Hoosier cabinet, using the drawers and shelves as steps, toppling the whole thing over on top of him and breaking all the dishes inside. Luckily David was not hurt, but when he told his teacher about the mishap the next day, she felt sorry for the family and took up a collection from the other parents, embarrassing Phyllis by presenting her with a new set of dishes.

One of the simple joys of life on the farm was riding in Dad's old truck to the elevator. Myron always said that he bought the trucks that other folks thought were already worn out. Bouncing along in the rusty red truck alongside Dad, the delicious smell of newly-mown hay drifting inside through the rolled-down windows, David felt like he was on top of the world. The truck's windshield was covered with random stickers that David collected and stuck there, a harmless boy's obsession that Myron didn't seem to mind. The men at the community elevator knew the family well and enjoyed talking to the children on their visits. The elevator smelled of old wood and corn and faint wisps of manure, the massive rusty grain bins a magical sight as the grain poured into a yellow mountain inside the truck bed. There were always old farmers hanging around, shooting the breeze and telling their tall farmers' tales. David loved the elevator, and especially tagging along with his dad.

David always tagged along with Myron, whether he wanted to or not. Sometimes it involved a lot of hard hot work, but sometimes it was just plain fun. While Myron was chopping corn for silage, David and his sisters liked to lie down in the wagon behind the tractor and let the chopped corn fall on top of them in a country-kids' version of "Chicken." The girls knew when it was getting too heavy and managed to crawl out before they were stuck, but not David. More than once, Myron had to stop the tractor and dig him out from under the warm, sharp load. Sometimes his stubbornness got way ahead of his brains.

As David lay in the hay mow on a lazy summer afternoon, looking across the fields toward the woods, even at his young age he knew life was good. Not simple, not easy, but very, very good.

CHAPTER 2

Country Girl

March, early 1970s

Baker Family Farm outside of Economy, Indiana

The crunch of manure-crusted boots plodding across the still-frozen ground broke the quiet, still air. While March had arrived and spring was supposedly just around the corner, today had felt much more like winter. Earl was tired, exhausted really. This time of year was a busy one on the farm; calving cows and farrowing sows brought extra work and extra worry, especially when the weather took a frigid turn like this. Despite the longer hours spent caring for his livestock, he loved this season. Something about the new life brought hope and promise for the year ahead.

Twisting the back doorknob, Earl heard her before he saw her. The soft, sweet medley of melodies sung in her high little girl voice never ceased to bring a smile to his face. After three sons and believing their family to be complete, God had blessed Earl Baker and his wife Patricia seven years later with a precious surprise: a darling baby girl on whom Earl doted every single day. Jennifer was an unexpected blessing to the seasoned farmer, and it was evident very early on that God had given Jenny a special gift, the voice of an angel. Earl's little angel.

Earl sat down on the bench to pull off his boots and barn clothes, savoring the delicious smells of dinner cooking with Jenny's music in the background. This was Earl's favorite time of day, a man's reward after many hard hours of work. He'd married a treasure in Patty, a wonderful cook and the best wife a farmer like him could hope to have.

Their courtship had begun very early, when both Earl and Patricia were young students at an elementary school in Webster, Indiana. Earl's school career got off to a shaky start, and even though he was two years older than Patricia, they ended up in the same grade by the time they reached high school. Patricia had her eyes and heart fixed on tall, handsome Earl from the start and even begged him to marry her before they graduated, but Earl was determined to finish school before taking a wife. His final year in high school he worked an eight-hour shift at a nearby roofing factory by night and then attended school by day. On May 8, 1948, the day following their graduation from Webster High School, Earl and Patricia exchanged wedding vows at the church his sister attended, St. John's Evangelical Lutheran Church in Richmond, Indiana. The newlyweds set up housekeeping in a small apartment house in Richmond. After a couple of moves and a two-year stint in California and Washington while Earl served as a cook in the United States Marine Corps, the Bakers eventually settled onto their own small family farm in rural Wayne County, Indiana.

Marrying his childhood sweetheart was the best decision Earl ever made, and he loved his wife with all his heart. She bore him three sons, Steve, Norman, and John, all great boys who labored hard alongside their dad on the farm. Earl knew he had been blessed beyond what a man like him deserved, and he never took any of them for granted. And then Jenny had come along. Granted, Earl and Pat were a bit taken aback at the thought of a new baby after the others were half-grown and already in school, but God had known best and Jenny's birth completed Earl's perfect little family and now he couldn't imagine life without her.

Earl smiled recollecting the days surrounding May 16, 1964, the day his Jennifer was born. Although her birth had been anticipated a couple of weeks earlier, Jennifer displayed very early on that she intended to do things her way and had waited to make her appearance until Earl was right in the middle of planting season. Thankfully Earl's family and friends pitched in and planted his cornfields for him while he tended to his wife and newborn daughter. Yes, Earl remembered, that was a day when his life changed forever. Who knew a tiny little girl could wrap her teeny fingers around his rough weathered ones and so quickly and easily worm her way into the heart of a tough farmer like himself?

Jenny adored her Daddy as much as he adored her. One day not too long ago, Jenny had bounced into the kitchen and proclaimed to her mommy, "When I grow up, I'm going to marry Daddy!" When Patricia had questioned how that was going to be possible, Jenny had the strategy all worked out in her little mind. "Well, I will be the Mommy and you can be my little girl."

Yes, Earl doted on his beautiful little curly-haired daughter, but they didn't always see eye to eye. If his Jenny was anything, she was strong-willed, and more than once she had gotten her dander up over something and decided to run away. One late afternoon, Earl was driving his tractor up the gravel lane toward the barn and he met Jenny flying on her tricycle as fast as her little legs could pedal. Earl had stopped the tractor and yelled at her to turn around and go on back to the house, but young Jenny never stopped pedaling. She'd almost reached the highway by the time her angry daddy drove up behind her in the family car, snatched her off the tricycle, tossed them both into the seat behind him, and drove her back home. She was a feisty one, his Jenny, and Earl secretly took an extra measure of pride in that knowledge.

His farm clothes off, Earl pushed his tall body upright and strode across the kitchen floor and pulled Patty into his arms for a quick squeeze, rubbing his strong hard knuckles up and down her back as he hugged her. His lovely wife smiled and relaxed into the familiar massage, finished off with a tender peck on the cheek from her man. Before even looking, Earl knew exactly where he'd find Jenny. Folded into her little rocking chair near the iron floor register, there she sat, the warm air coaxing her dark curls to dance around her down-turned face, cuddling a tiny baby snugly wrapped in a doll blanket. Most little girls would be holding and serenading a baby doll, but Earl knew that Jenny's baby wasn't a doll at all.

The round, wrinkled, speckled nose poked out of the blanket and saw Earl before Jenny even looked up. Engrossed as she was in her mission, Jenny hadn't yet noticed that her daddy had come into the house. The runty piglet wiggled and then little Jenny raised her head too, grinning at Earl as she continued singing. She gently unwrapped the baby pig, half-asleep and cozy with his tummy full, and gently put him back in the box next to the register before jumping out of her tiny rocker.

"Daddy!" Jenny cried, as she wrapped her arms around Earl's long legs. Earl picked up his young daughter, half-tossing her into the air as she giggled with delight.

"How's the new baby doing?" Earl asked. Jenny had always had a fondness for those runt pigs, the ones that weren't robust and strong like their siblings and often were abandoned and left to die by the mother sow. It was the cruel way of the barnyard, survival of the fittest. But soft-hearted Earl couldn't stand to just let nature take its course, so he'd bring the weak, neglected piggies inside where Jenny loved to bottle-feed them and nurse them back to health. Often, under Jenny's tender loving care, those rejected pigs would grow up to be just as strong and healthy as their littermates.

"Isn't he just the cutest little thing, Daddy? I think he's going to be just fine." And Earl didn't doubt her. When it came to nursing helpless and abandoned babies back to health, his Jenny knew what she was doing.

Jennifer Baker, 7 years old   1970

"Suppertime." Pat called to her family from the kitchen, and Earl gently set Jenny back down on the linoleum floor and the two of them headed to the bathroom to wash their hands. Not only did Pat cook delicious and nutritious meals for her family, but she loved to bake and did so nearly every day. Daily desserts were the norm, and early on Jenny developed her sweet tooth. The family always sat down for meals together, and Earl relished those moments with his family around the table, the perfect ending to a day well-lived.

He was blessed. Very, very blessed.

A few years later, on a hot July day

Same farmhouse

Sweat trickled down the back of her neck as Jenny guided her pig across the barn lot. With the Wayne County 4-H Fair just a few days away, there weren't many more practice sessions before she'd be showing her pig for real in front of the judges. Jenny's brothers had showed cattle in 4-H, a much easier task in many ways since one could put a lead rope on a calf. But Jenny had always been much fonder of the pigs, even though sometimes it was frustrating trying to prod them in the right direction. One couldn't put a lead rope on a pig; control was all in the subtle and skilled use of the show cane.

Jenny relished the challenge though, and the pigs cooperated with her most of the time. Perhaps it was her soothing voice that coaxed them into obedience, but Jenny knew they remembered her from their early days. Pigs were smart, much smarter than folks gave them credit for, and Jenny and her pigs seemed to have a mutual understanding and an unusual bond.

While most young girls on the cusp of womanhood preferred being inside learning domestic skills, Jenny didn't. She'd much rather be outside, helping on the farm. Jenny had no interest in learning how to cook or clean or sew, but instead whenever she heard Earl's tractor engine firing, she'd dash out the door to ride along. Even helping to bale hay in the sweltering Indiana summer heat beat pretty much anything she might be doing inside the house. Shadowing her father, Jenny learned all about tools and how to fix things, and Earl taught his daughter how to drive the tractor, which she adored. Living on the farm, there were always plenty of chores to do -- animals to be fed and watered, eggs to be gathered from the henhouse (even if it meant warding off the mean rooster with a big stick!), weeds to be pulled from the garden. Jenny was usually eager to help with them all, a country girl through and through.

With few nearby neighbors, the Bakers were fairly isolated on their dead-end gravel road, but Jenny didn't mind. Content playing alone much of the time, after she was in school she did have a good friend who lived just up the road from her house. Sandy shared Jenny's love of anything outside, and the two of them had many adventures together catching crawdads in the creek, picking apples from the orchard, riding bicycles down the dirt country roads -- anything that the two tomboys could do together outside. Sandy and Jenny were the best of friends and spent many summer hours together, even playing summer softball together although Jenny quickly discovered she was not much of a softball player. The girls' love for all things outdoors and disdain for more "womanly" housekeeping skills caused their mothers to more than once wonder whether their daughters might never learn how to be ladies.

Besides being outside, Jenny had one other love. Music. Music was joy in her life, singing her meditation and therapy. God had gifted her with an amazing musical instrument in her voice, and one of the happiest days of Jenny's young life was when she got another musical instrument, her very own piano. It found its home in their small dining room, and Jenny began taking piano lessons during her elementary years. Jenny's greatest desire was to sing, and being able to accompany herself on the piano was her dream. More than once she frustrated Mrs. Doerstler, her piano teacher, by turning up her nose at the classical pieces she was assigned, much preferring more popular tunes to which she could sing along. Jenny disdained the required daily practice sessions, but with her parents' encouragement she continued taking lessons for a few years, getting off the school bus at the Doerstler home for her weekly lessons, until her skills were adequate to be her own pianist as she sang.

It was through her gift of song that Jenny first began attending church. Although she loved attending Sugar Grove Community Church's annual Vacation Bible School each summer, the Bakers weren't a church-going family. The family that owned the farm where Earl worked and lived didn't allow any farming to be done on Sundays, so for Jenny and her brothers Sunday became a day to sleep in and later clean their rooms.

One day Mrs. Rice, her fifth-grade school teacher, invited Jenny to come sing during a church service at Sugar Grove. Jenny didn't know it at the time, but she would later learn that Mrs. Rice had been faithfully praying for a long time that the Baker family would come to know the Lord. That first day she sang at church was a day that changed Jenny's life forever, because after that she began to go to church regularly. Church was a chance to do what she loved most, to sing, and she enjoyed it so much that as a preteen she even joined the adult choir. Earl would drop his daughter off at church Sunday mornings and come back to pick her up after services were over, once in a great while staying for the service just so he could hear her sing.

When Jenny had been going to church for about a year, the church's youth leader Howard Addison was speaking and suddenly a loud alarm went off inside the church. Mr. Addison suddenly and without warning collapsed, falling on the floor. Jenny was terrified, thinking that he was dead! Mr. Addison's well-orchestrated illustration had served its purpose, for when he got up and began quoting a passage from I Corinthians 15, "*...in a flash, in the twinkling of an eye... For the trumpet will sound, the dead will be raised imperishable, and we will be changed,*" Jenny was convicted and her heart changed right then and there. She soaked up every word of the sermon, hearing and believing that Jesus came to die for her sins and those who loved Jesus would live with him forever. During the closing hymn and altar call, Jenny could not stay in her pew and ran up the aisle to the front of the church, at eleven years old sincerely dedicating her life to Jesus at that very moment. A few months later, Jenny was baptized in her pastor Max Knight's backyard swimming pool, witnessed by her parents, who did not attend church at that time, as well as by her new godparents Howard Addison and Norma Rice. It was one of the happiest moments of Jenny's life.

From that time on, Jenny rarely missed a Sunday and eagerly absorbed and treasured all the knowledge she could about God and His saving grace. Eventually, Jenny's dedication to the Lord and her faithful attendance at Sugar Grove rubbed off on her parents. Earl himself had an incredible singing voice which caught listeners completely off-guard when they heard his gorgeous soprano melodies coming from the mouth of a big, strong hog farmer. When he began to sing duets with Jenny at church, Earl learned he enjoyed worshiping at the little country church and especially singing with his captivating daughter. Nothing pleased Jenny more than singing songs of worship with her father as her mother beamed from a nearby pew, and while Earl and Pat didn't attend quite as faithfully as Jenny, they did nonetheless become somewhat regulars at Sugar Grove.

Being a small, rural congregation situated in the middle of Indiana farm fields, the weekly attendees were predictably the same.

So when, one Sunday, a young African-American couple with several beautiful little brown-skinned children walked through the church doors and found a seat in the tiny sanctuary, heads turned. It wasn't that the family was anything but welcome, just simply that Sugar Grove folks didn't run into many black folks in their daily lives. No one from the church had yet greeted them when teenaged Jenny boldly but gently approached them and volunteered to take their squirmy littlest one to the church nursery. As the frustrated, grateful parents trustingly handed over the fussy child into the arms of this friendly stranger, Jenny's gift of comforting and caring for babies in distress quickly soothed the little one. Decades later her father Earl would note that this small, loving gesture was itself a remarkable foretelling of things God had in store for Jenny's future.

Farm life suited Jenny as much as she suited it, everything about it. But more than anything, Jenny adored the animals. Not only did she nurse the runt pigs back to health, Jenny often bottle-fed newborn Angus calves when their mothers couldn't or wouldn't nurse them. Dipping the powdered milk out of the big bag into the calves' bottles, Jenny lovingly mixed in water and giggled as the calves came running at the sight of Jenny, poking their muzzles between the fence rails, clamoring for their meals. Holding tightly to the bottles, she sang to them as they vigorously sucked down the milky mixture until white, bubbly slobbers ran out of the corners of their little mouths. Mothering was in Jenny's blood, and those abandoned farm babies were lucky to have such a capable mother-substitute.

Actually, there wasn't much on the farm that intimidated Jenny. She'd grown from a little girl, helping her daddy get the hogs in for feeding, opening and closing gates, and fetching tools (while Earl repaired all the things that constantly broke on the farm) into a strong teenage girl who would hold pigs while Earl castrated them and who could stack straw bales in the hay mow as high and solid as anyone. As her brothers loaded the bales onto the elevator below, Jenny would grab them by the twine and snag them off one by one from her station at the very top of the old barn. Standing just inside the open window,

Jenny would carry the sweet-smelling golden bales across the worn wooden planks of the hay mow floor and carefully stack them in the exact way that Earl had prescribed. Although it was stifling and dusty up there near the barn rafters in the middle of the summer, Jenny knew her momma would reward them with homemade milkshakes and warm cookies when their hot task was finished, and she never complained.

Well, almost never complained. Her brothers swore innocence when, one day, Jenny reached to grab a bale and a snake very much still alive was lashing out its wiggly angry head at her, its long tail caught up so tightly in the bale that it couldn't escape. Jenny's blood-curdling screams, whether her brothers expected them or not, could be heard all over the farm and years later would still give oldest brother Steve a chuckle as he retold the familiar tale. But Jenny was undaunted, unwilling to let a little snake get the best of her even then.

Charlie Brown, the family dog, followed Jenny wherever she went. And there was always a never-ending supply of barn kittens, entertaining Jenny with their playful antics and purring contentedly as she coddled them. Nurturing small and innocent creatures was just instinctive to Jenny, and she had plenty of opportunities there on the farm.

But things weren't always picture-perfect at the Baker home. Strong-willed Jenny, as is many times the case with teenage girls, clashed often and hard with her mother. Pat had her own personal struggles. The sudden and untimely death of her own father had catapulted Pat into a deep and very dark depression, just unable to deal with the tragedy. She relied on Jenny's help more and more, and as much as Jenny preferred her outdoor chores, she found herself having to shoulder the household responsibilities, learning to cook and care for the home to keep the family going. When Pat was eventually hospitalized for several months, Jenny kept the home fires burning. As a pre-teen, Jenny didn't really know what was wrong, just that her mom was sick, and she did what needed to be done.

Adding to that the normal struggles and hormones of an independent teenage girl, Jenny's high school years were at times tumultuous. Those seasons were difficult ones, not only for Earl and Pat and the boys, but especially for Jenny. In hindsight Jenny would realize that those years molded and shaped her, strengthening her mentally and spiritually, but as she was living through them they were anything but pleasant.

But between those tough seasons were many wonderful seasons, times that the adult Jenny would remember with fondness. She learned so many lessons on the farm, and looking back years later realized that all along God had been teaching and preparing her for a work she could never have imagined. Hers was a childhood that would serve her well in the years to come.

Taking a break from her farm chores, Jenny sat on her favorite low-hanging branch up in an old shade tree in the yard, dangling and swinging her long legs in the breeze on a lazy summer afternoon, soaking up the warm sunrays and watching the clouds change shapes as they floated across the bright blue sky. Even at her young age Jenny knew her simple life here in the country was good. Not simple, not easy, but very, very good.

CHAPTER 3

Beginnings

January 1980

Baker Farm, Economy, Indiana

Jenny's bright hazel eyes stared back at her from the bathroom mirror. She fluffed her long dark curls for the umpteenth time, checking once more her make-up and teeth, satisfied that the outfit she'd chosen looked good on her tall, slim body. First impressions were important and she intended to make a good one.

Bouncing back to the living room, she anxiously pulled aside the curtains and glanced through the frosted windowpanes down the gravel lane. Still nothing. Jenny took another deep breath and her tanned hands dropped the hemmed fabric edge. Her suntan, certainly an unusual sight in the middle of a Hoosier winter, hadn't yet faded, even though memories of swaying palm trees already seemed light years away from the white, frigid landscape on the other side of this window. It had been her first trip outside the Midwest, an unexpected surprise compliments of her deceased aunt who'd left Patty enough money to finance their dream trip to Hawaii. Earl, Patty, and Jenny had enjoyed most of last month in the tropical paradise, and they had returned home well-rested and sun-kissed.

Giddy with nervous excitement, Jenny paced through the house, caught between re-checking out the window and re-checking her reflection in the mirror. Peering through either glass, she wasn't quite sure what she was looking for, but Jenny knew her blind date would be arriving soon and she was anxious to meet this man that Sandy had so highly recommended.

Just fifteen years old, this certainly wasn't her first date. Jenny, at the halfway mark of her sophomore year in high school, had already had more than her share of boyfriend experiences for her tender age. Patty's season of depression in Jenny's early teen years not only caused Jenny to grow up much more quickly than normal, but the extra burden of his wife's illness preoccupied Earl, and he was just too busy to keep too close an eye on his attractive young daughter. Jenny was a good girl and he trusted her.

Earl knew all too well the extra work Jenny was shouldering, but he had plenty on his plate as well. With his wife ill and the farm to run, Earl had more than his own share of stress. As much as he wished things were different, there didn't seem to be much choice except to keep plugging along as best they all could. Jenny was a trooper, and many times Earl's heart lurched with feelings of tender helplessness as he heard his daughter's sweet voice singing in the kitchen. Sometimes if the spirit hit, Earl would join in, the two of them creating an impromptu duet which lightened both of their moods.

Although Earl adored his daughter, raising a teenage girl alone was a daunting task, especially for a man much more comfortable castrating pigs and harvesting corn than dealing with pubescent female drama. No doubt he was a bit lax enforcing rules for his daughter, but beyond the normal emotional roller-coaster that accompanies hormonal teen girls, Jenny seemed to be doing just fine.

So Earl hadn't thought it unusual that Jenny had started dating so young. After all, she was beautiful and talented and not surprisingly turned a lot of immature male heads. Boys had come and gone in the past few years, nothing to worry about. Not a man to borrow trouble,

Earl coped by keeping busy and overlooking much of what went on around him, convincing himself that soon enough this season too would pass and Pat would be well and life could get back to normal.

Jenny had only agreed to this blind date when Sandy had begged her best friend to double-date with her and her boyfriend Kent, who happened to be one of David's best friends. Having recently come out of a bad break-up with her latest beau, Jenny was a bit leery about going out with a man nearly four years older than her, someone she had never even met. She'd seen a photo of David, thinking him very handsome with his thick blond hair, big smile, and brilliant blue eyes, and that had certainly piqued her interest. Jenny knew that her school classmate Trecia, David's younger sister, wasn't any too eager for her brother to go out with Jenny. But Trecia's reluctance didn't deter Jenny, as she chalked it up to being protective of her big brother. Jenny trusted Sandy…certainly her best friend wouldn't fix her up with a loser!

A knock at the front door. HE WAS HERE! Apparently occupied by her thoughts, Jenny had somehow missed seeing his car arrive. Even though she'd been expecting it, the knock caught her off guard and she willed her heart to stop racing as she walked to answer the door, Patty following a few steps behind her.

Jenny wasn't disappointed. David was as cute as she'd imagined him and, for reasons she couldn't quite put her finger on, Jenny found that the fact he was wearing cowboy boots pleased her. Jenny invited him inside, and when Jenny introduced to him her mom, the words came out of David's mouth before he could stop them. "Hi, Mom," he said, his nerves causing him to misspeak and create a brief awkwardness in the room until Pat gave him a puzzled smile, breaking the ice. That initial meeting would not be forgotten and over the years would become somewhat of a family joke.

David wasn't disappointed either. In fact, he was quite wowed by this bronze beauty that stood before him! David, now 19, had himself recently come out of a very painful break-up and he certainly wasn't looking to begin another relationship any time soon. He'd reluctantly agreed to this blind date as well, caving to the pressure from his close friend Kent. Always up for a good time, at this point that's all that interested David. A fun double-date with their best friends, nothing more.

Bidding her parents farewell and pulling the door closed behind them, David followed Jenny down the porch steps and opened the car door for her. Kent and Sandy were already in the back seat, talking and giggling and quite proud of themselves for successfully setting up this evening. Conversation was easy, and soon the four friends were chatting their way down the highway.

Taking Jenny by surprise, David pulled into the small parking lot of the Losantville Package Store and he and Kent got out and walked inside. Sandy could hardly wait until the car doors slammed shut so she could ask Jenny what she thought of David, secretly pleased with herself for having done her part in bringing the two of them together. Jenny thought it was a bit odd to be picking up liquor before the date had even begun, but David and Kent were older and presumably wiser and who was she to question them when the two under-legal-aged teenagers emerged a few minutes later carrying a bottle of Peppermint Schnapps?

The foursome made the twenty-mile drive to the nearby city of Muncie, filling up with all-you-can-eat crab legs at Cactus Charlie's before hitting the movie theater and laughing their way through Steve Martin's hit flick "The Jerk." Stopping along a deserted country road before taking their dates back to their respective homes for the night, the men popped open the liquor and passed it around. Jenny took a sip and thought it tasted terrible, but David and Kent seemed to enjoy the contents of that bottle enough for all of them.

The liquor gone and the new day already beginning, reluctantly David turned his car back toward Economy to drop Jenny off. Escorting her to her back door, David wrapped his arm around her to ward off her shivering in the freezing January air and, emboldened by the alcohol, surprised even himself by kissing her good-night. He couldn't wipe the smile off his face as he sauntered back to the car. It had been a good evening, yes, a good evening indeed.

Earl and Pat had long since retired to bed by the time Jenny arrived home in the wee Sunday morning hours. Farm life didn't allow them late nights. Jenny watched the tail lights disappear down the gravel driveway, then she quietly went inside and softly closed the wooden door behind her. And she smiled all the way up the stairs.

Easter, Spring 1980

The past three months had been some of the happiest of Jenny's life. She had fallen head-over-heels for Dave, and she knew he was smitten with her as well. Her weekday hours were filled with school and sports, but her thoughts were never far from her new boyfriend. She lived for the weekends when they could spend time together, often double-dating with Kent and Sandy to dinner and a movie, or playing board games with Dave's sister Mariellen and her husband Brad.

Since they were classmates at small Hagerstown High School, Jenny knew Trecia, who had by now warmed up to the fact that Jenny was dating her big brother. Jenny had spent some time with Mariellen and Brad, as well as briefly meeting Dave's parents at White Branch Church, where she'd taken to occasionally singing specials during the Sunday worship service. But the other five siblings were still strangers to Jenny, and she certainly had never had the opportunity to be with them all at once until that first Easter she and Dave were together.

Sunday family dinners were the rule with the Bell clan, and extra-special get-togethers when holidays rolled around. Since Dave was next to the youngest child, most of his brothers and sisters were already married and many had children of their own. So when the

Bells got together at Phyllis and Myron's with all eight siblings and their families in attendance, it was a gathering to behold. When Dave brought Jenny to join the family for Easter dinner, Jenny was understandably intimidated and a bit overwhelmed. She'd never seen so many relatives together in one place! A noisy, happy chaos filled the air, and Dave led Jenny from one person to another, introducing her as she desperately tried to connect all the twigs and branches on this large family tree. Nervously she smiled and graciously greeted each one, then politely found a nice quiet viewing spot on the perimeter of the happy crowd and sat herself down.

Surveying the busy family around her, Jenny's eyes kept returning to the young children, cousins still wearing their Easter best chasing each other across the newly-green grass in the warm spring sunshine. Always drawn to children, Jenny slowly began interacting with them and was soon joining in their games. The children delighted in their new playmate, and it was through her love for the family's littlest ones that Jenny won the hearts of their parents and the rest of the Bells. Dave beamed as he watched his new sweetheart laughing and singing with his young nieces and nephews, and he once again realized that this Jenny was someone very special.

But she was still so young and had two full years of high school left. Dave had graduated from Hagerstown High School two years earlier and was learning the tool and die trade hands-on under the tutelage of Marion Shore, running the metal lathe at Marion's business Magna Machine and Tool. Not a very serious student in high school, Dave had always assumed his future would be in farming and never had any interest in furthering his education beyond his high school diploma. He had worked on his cousin Bill's dairy farm during his senior year, and then took a brief stint traveling across the country with a local doctor who owned a dairy farm and was on the dairy cattle show circuit. After incessantly begging Marion to hire him to do odd jobs in the shop, Dave was now quickly learning that business and squirreling his money away for his eventual farming endeavors.

Dave soon discovered he had a talent and passion for the tool and die trade. Having not advanced in math classes beyond freshman algebra, Dave taught himself the necessary trigonometry skills on the job. Marion was a good boss and mentor to young Dave, who thrived and succeeded at Magna, working his way up the ranks and earning more responsibility, soaking up knowledge about all the different aspects of the business along the way. Early on in his career at Magna, Marion gave Dave the responsibility of a project to build a luggage rack for some missionaries in Haiti. While Dave was eager to please his boss, as he worked on the luggage rack Dave couldn't help but think the whole situation to be a crazy waste of time and effort. It was another glimpse of the mission thread God was already weaving through Dave's life tapestry, one he wouldn't see until many years down the road.

But for now, here he was, a successfully employed adult who found himself in love with a girl, although wise beyond her years, who was still in high school.

Dave wasn't a stranger to romance himself. Just a few short weeks prior to meeting Jenny, Dave had gone through a very nasty and painful break-up with a girlfriend who had just gotten too serious too quickly. As was the custom in their small community, Dave had given the local girl his senior key to wear around her neck as a token of their steady-dating status and, broken-hearted and angry, she had not returned it to him when he split with her. After they had been dating a few weeks and Jenny felt herself established as Dave's new girlfriend, she confronted her rival at school about the senior key and eventually got into a fight with Dave's former flame, retrieving the key and proudly clasping it around her own neck.

When Dave noticed Jenny wearing his senior key, a silent alarm went off in his head. Not again! He wasn't ready to go steady with anyone. All he wanted was someone with whom he could have fun, someone to date with no strings attached. Jenny seemed to have other plans and he had to admit those plans scared him a little, so he took the necessary risk of losing her and made his feelings known to Jenny. She listened intently and understandingly as he explained his stance, but secretly dug in her heart's heels even deeper. Although she hadn't yet shared it with anyone, Jenny knew in her heart that Dave was the man she would marry. She would win him over.

And she did. That first Christmas Dave presented Jenny with a promise ring, and from that point on the two of them settled into God's apparent plans for them to spend the rest of their lives together. But all that would have to wait until Jenny graduated from high school.

Jenny was smart, but she didn't seem to care much about her school work. Bringing home average grades suited Jenny just fine, as she had neither desire nor plans to continue her education after high school, especially now that a future with Dave lay before her. But as much as she disdained academics, Jenny thrived in sports and the performing arts. Tall and athletic, Jenny filled her after-school hours playing on the school volleyball and basketball teams. And while sports were fun and kept her busy, what Jenny really loved most was drama and singing. Whenever the school put on a play, Jenny was always a part of it. And she often thought that choir was what kept her half-way interested in school.

Dave never missed a game or performance, and it never failed to give Jenny a thrill to see his smiling face cheering approval from the audience. He was her biggest fan, and she his, the two of them loving each other with all of their hearts. Even though both were busy, oftentimes those days and weeks seemed to drag on oh-so-long as they were both eager to begin their life together.

Jenny's senior year couldn't go fast enough. By this time she was totally over school and homework and took only two classes that last semester, the required US Government and her beloved Choir, just enough to give her the minimum credits to graduate. She took a part-time job in the local print shop, binding books and doing odd print jobs. And the rest of her free time she spent planning her wedding.

Many times daily Jenny would find herself smiling at the diamond engagement ring on her finger. She and Dave had picked it out together, along with matching wedding bands which would soon join the diamond on her finger. Dave had gifted her with a wooden Hope Chest just that past Christmas, and Jenny and Pat had been steadily placing inside lovely household linens and other items both delicate and useful, following a timeworn tradition of many brides-to-be from generations past.

Their plans and dreams were about to become reality, the beginnings of a real life roller-coaster ride, the likes of which neither of them could have ever begun to imagine. Buckle up, hang on, and get ready to lick and turn.

CHAPTER 4

From This Day Forward

June 1982

Poconos Mountain Resort in Pennsylvania

From his vantage point, life was perfect. Gazing into the night heavens studded with a gazillion stars and listening to the quiet sounds of mountain darkness, snuggling his new bride Jenny as they lounged together in the warm waters of their heart-shaped private pool, Dave couldn't stop smiling. He was one blessed man, and he knew it.

What an exciting whirlwind the past few days, even weeks, had been! Jenny's graduation from Hagerstown High School in late May had been quickly followed by finalizing wedding preparations. After waiting for what had seemed like an insufferably long two years, it had been hard to comprehend that the day for which the two of them had dreamed and planned had finally arrived.

Saturday, June 19, 1982.

Jenny and Dave had awakened to a rainy morning, but the summer sun quickly chased the clouds away, turning the soggy morning into a glorious June day. The showers had scrubbed the air clean and the sky a perfectly clear sapphire blue. Dave drove out to the Baker farm to help prepare for the evening's celebratory hog roast. As he helped Earl and his sons set up tables and chairs in the farmhouse yard for the festivities, Dave often glanced back toward the house hoping to get a quick glimpse of his soon-to-be wife. Tradition told him that it was bad luck for the groom and bride to see each other before the ceremony that day, but Dave couldn't help be just a tiny bit disappointed when Jenny took extra pains to stay out of his sight all morning.

She, after all, had plenty of preparations to do herself. Jenny and Patty were busy in the house, Patty prepping food to be served later and Jenny doing last-minute honeymoon packing before getting herself all prettied up for the wedding. Patty and Jenny had worked diligently for this special day, and every detail had been thought about and carefully worked through. It was going to be the perfect day!

Earlier that morning, Patty and Jenny had dressed up Sugar Grove Community Church with flowers and bows befitting the occasion. The small church would, in just a few hours, be overflowing with family and friends. Max Knight, pastor of the church and family friend, would be the officiant on this most important day of her life. The evening before, the wedding party had rehearsed the ceremony and everyone knew what they were supposed to do and when they were supposed to do it. Or they thought they did. Jenny smiled to herself. She wouldn't have to keep her secret much longer. She could hardly wait to see Dave's reaction to her big surprise!

An hour prior to the wedding, all those involved in the wedding were there at the church, antsy for the ceremony to begin. As the music played, the guests were seated, with Phyllis and Myron and Patty the last to be ushered down the aisle to the front pews. On cue, Pastor Knight came through the front side door followed by Dave, his Best Man (and best friend) Kent, and groomsmen brother Chuck and his friend Glen. They lined up facing the gathered crowd and watched as bridesmaids Mary Jane and Brenda, Jenny's close friends, made their way slowly down the aisle looking lovely in their floor-length light blue dresses. Jenny's best friend Sandy was her Maid of Honor and the final member of the wedding party to walk down the aisle, building the anticipation for the appearance of the bride.

Dave discreetly tugged at the lapel of his white tux, tiny beads of sweat already appearing on his forehead in the humid heat of the sanctuary. This was it, the moment he'd been waiting for all of his life. He couldn't wipe the smile off his face as he kept his blue eyes peeled toward the doors at the back of the church, awaiting the arrival of his bride.

After a short pause, the music began once again. Wait…the wrong song was playing! He threw a panicked glance over his shoulder at the organist, hoping she'd recognized her error. But she kept right on playing, obviously oblivious to the blunder. And then, just as Dave wondered what was going to happen, he heard it.

That voice! He'd know it anywhere, that angelic voice was filling the church with its perfect melody and melting his heart at the same time. Dave felt tears spilling onto his cheeks as he realized it wasn't a mistake at all. Jenny was singing to him, sharing her love through her magical voice on their wedding day. And Dave thought his heart would burst with love as the old wooden doors opened and he watched Earl escort his ravishing daughter down the aisle toward him, singing and smiling all the way. What a beautiful, touching start to their life together!

The warm pool water gently rippled around Dave as he remembered. The joy he'd felt that

Wedding Day, June 19, 1982

- 37 -

day and in the days since was a joy he'd never known possible. He turned his head to look at Jenny quietly relaxed in his arms, her eyes closed but a wisp of a contented smile on her face. Over the past couple of days they had relived each moment of their wedding day, sharing memories and laughing over stories that would forever make that day unforgettable.

After Jenny's stunning musical surprise, the wedding ceremony itself was traditional and fairly unremarkable, except when Chuck knocked over the candelabra and for a brief moment Dave had wondered if anyone had ever burned down a church during a wedding ceremony. When Dave's kiss of his new bride put the exclamation mark on the vows, the happy crowd of well-wishers bustled into the church's fellowship area for wedding cake and mints before driving out to the Baker farm for a supper of home-raised barbequed pork and all the fixings.

When darkness had settled on the Baker farm and the guests had bid Dave and Jenny best wishes and headed home to their beds, Dave loaded Jenny's suitcase beside his own onto the back seat of Dave's car and the young couple drove the ten miles or so to Richmond, just inside the Ohio state line. It was there they spent their first night as husband and wife, and their life together had begun.

After telephone calls to both of their dads to wish them a Happy Father's Day the following Sunday morning, Dave and Jenny were back in the car and on their way to honeymoon in Pennsylvania's Pocono Mountains. Dave, always the planner and organizer, had enjoyed making sure all the details of this first trip together would be perfect. He had chosen a couples' resort getaway, complete with this heart-shaped pool in which they were now luxuriating, excited to get off to a fabulous and romantic start with his new bride. Years later, they joked that the resort's accommodations and atmosphere were a bit on the cheesy side, but through the prism of their newlywed eyes at the time it was indeed a sweetly romantic way to begin their married life.

Neither of them had ever seen mountains or traveled extensively, and they snapped photo after photo of mountain scenery, awed at this landscape that was so different from their flat Indiana homeland. By the end of the week it was time to head home, the newlyweds stopping at Hershey, Pennsylvania on their way home to tour the chocolate-famed city.

All too soon, the honeymoon was over and real life set in. When they arrived home, the couple set up housekeeping in a mobile home that Dave had purchased a few months before. Sited on a rented lot out in the country along Buck Creek Pike, it was small and modest but cozy, adequate for the young couple. Dave had gone back to work at Magna and Jen at the Hagerstown Exponent's print shop, and they quickly settled down into their new life together.

During the week, they were reliable and hard workers. Dave had earned the respect of his boss and was moving up the Magna ranks very quickly, his salary moving up with him. With the two of them employed and living rather modestly in their trailer, Dave and Jen happily found themselves with extra money which they enjoyed spending frivolously on weekend trips to party with some friends down on the Ohio River, riding motorcycles, frequent vacations, and new cars. It didn't take long for Dave's credit card balance to build up, but Dave had no problem paying the monthly minimum payment and at this point so early in their marriage Jen was not aware of their financial details, trusting Dave knew how to handle their money.

Mounting debt didn't slow Dave down in the least. He was loving life in the fast lane, making too much money for his own good but spending every last dime before he'd even earned it. Add to that a zest for social drinking and even a brief dabbling into drugs, and the combination was a disaster just waiting to happen. Working hard and partying harder, Dave was convinced they were living the American dream, and Jen was blissfully unaware of the deep financial pit into which they were burying themselves.

Jen had already delayed their marriage longer than she had wanted, and she didn't want to wait to start a family with the man she loved. Eager to become a mother, Jen found herself pregnant soon after the honeymoon. How elated they both were at the thought of a new baby of their very own! And how absolutely devastated they both were when, just a few weeks into the pregnancy, Jen miscarried.

Faced with seemingly unbearable grief, Jen was overcome with deep sadness and Dave medicated his pain with alcohol and spending sprees. As the weeks and months passed, their grief gradually dimmed as their mountain of debt grew.

And Dave soon found himself having a lot of difficulty licking and turning quickly enough.

CHAPTER 5

Living the Dream

June 1995

Indiana

"Never Africa. The ONLY reason I'd EVER go to Africa is to hunt."

A nervous chuckle rippled through the room. Holding up his crude sketch of the African continent, Dave had never been more serious as he scanned the faces of new friends, fellow Christian men who were all winding up a refreshing and inspiring weekend together at the Brethren Way of Christ. A time of encouragement and rededication to the faith, the weekend had touched Dave deeply. He had come very close to skipping the retreat altogether, but when a big order for the business had fallen through at the last minute he no longer had a valid excuse not to go. So reluctantly Dave had gone, and during the course of the weekend God had touched his mind and stirred his heart deeply. In his sharing he had dedicated not only himself but also Cutting Edge, his brand new business, to God.

Now the weekend was nearly over and the leader had posed the question to the men…where would you most NOT want to go if you felt God calling you there? Dave hadn't hesitated a moment. He'd definitely been feeling God's call to share God's Word more intentionally, but to whom and where he hadn't given much thought. Sure, he'd be willing and even eager to go on mission trips in other parts of the world if God asked.

But Africa??? No way! Although the thought of a unique hunting trophy to display on his farmhouse living room wall was a little tempting…

Dave left the final meeting, packed up and threw his bag of belongings in the truck, and headed home. While he'd thoroughly enjoyed his weekend retreat, he was ready to be home with Jen and his two boys. It was a lovely spring day, and as he drove south from North Webster across the green, awakening Indiana countryside, Dave had plenty of time to think. And wonder. And be very, very thankful.

Cutting Edge was off to a great start! His dream of having his own precision metal-cutting business had come true just a few months before. Located just 200 yards or so behind their home, the new business had hit the ground running. The contacts Dave had made in his lifetime in the Hagerstown area led to many orders right from the start, and things in the shop were busy. So busy, in fact, that Dave had felt guilty about leaving for the weekend to attend this retreat, but now he was so glad he had. It had been a much-needed refreshment to his stagnant faith walk, and the fellowship time and sharing with other Christian men had been uplifting and nothing short of amazing.

Until that final session. For some reason, Dave just couldn't shake the silent nagging of that question…and his answer.

Pulling off of Indiana highway 38 into his driveway, Dave smiled. How good it felt to be home! Since moving into the old, beautiful farmhouse just over two years ago, Dave and Jen had done lots of remodeling and it was slowly becoming the home of their dreams. They had rented it at first, then made it their own in 1993. While there were still lots of projects to be started and completed, slowly the homestead was making the transition, and Dave and Jen could see themselves happy and content there for years and years to come.

Down a lane just behind the home sat the shop. Clearing the legal and zoning hurdles and getting it up and running had been no small feat, but lately things had settled down and the fledgling business was doing well. Looking back, Dave saw that God's fingerprints had been all over the business long before he realized it. The lessons Dave had learned and the connections Dave had made at Magna, the experience and unique training he had received at Star in Columbus, as well as during his brief stint managing the Academy Wire Services shop in nearby Knightstown had all served him well. The orders were pouring in and his customer base growing quickly. God had certainly blessed this new venture!

Seeing their dad's truck pull into the driveway, Chris and Nate ran out into the yard to greet Dave. One after another, Dave hugged his young boys and swung them into the air to their delight. Smiling, Dave picked them both up and carried them into the house where Jen met the three of them with hugs all around. Yes, it was good to be home.

looking back....

After the tragedy of the miscarriage early in their marriage, God had blessed Dave and Jen beyond their imaginings eighteen months later when Christopher Maurice was born April 7, 1984. He'd given them more than a few scary moments with newborn breathing issues and had come home from the hospital with an apnea monitor, but Dave fondly remembered how excited he had been to pick up his wife and newborn son at the hospital in a brand new Honda station wagon that he'd just bought as a surprise for Jen. It was an extravagance that they didn't need and an expense they really couldn't afford, but wasn't his new growing family worth it? Dave had justified the purchase and Jen was too immersed in her motherly contentment to question it as they happily drove home to their Buck Creek Pike mobile home.

It hadn't taken long for that mobile home to feel cramped, and when Chris was just a few months old they sold the trailer and moved into a rental farmhouse several miles away on Highway 1. The big old house had lots more room and was closer to work for both of them. Jen had never been happier; she adored her new baby boy and her new role. Motherhood suited her perfectly.

But as she spent those first weeks home recovering and adjusting to motherhood, slowly she began to discover that the pieces of their family financial situation just didn't quite fit together like she had assumed. The daily trip to the mailbox would often bring bills, bills to which she hadn't paid much attention until now. Dave had always taken care of paying them and she'd never felt the need to know. But when she noticed the large and growing balances they were consistently carrying on their credit cards, slowly it dawned on her that things weren't adding up, and she soon realized that they were up to their eyeballs in debt.

Not that Dave had hidden it from her, as he himself hadn't yet realized that they were digging themselves into a deeper and deeper financial pit. All those vacations, boats, motorcycles, and new cars he extravagantly bought every year did not come without consequences. Yes, Dave was bringing home a very good income from Magna, but their financial hole was so deep it was going to take a long time to pay their way out. Dave and Jen decided together that she needed to pursue more lucrative employment, and soon she left the Exponent print shop and landed a job selling cars at a Richmond dealership.

It turned out to be a perfect fit for the new mother. She'd drop little Chris off to stay with his grandmother Pat, who by this time had given her life to Jesus and was living free of the mental suffering that had tortured her for years before, and drive her company-issued car to the dealership. Not only was having a woman salesperson on staff unusual at the time, Jen had a unique way with her customers and discovered quickly that her soft-sell techniques endeared her especially to women buyers. Having always been interested in cars, Jen knew her stuff and could hold her own talking engines and drive trains with the best of the male salesmen, and her easy manner and lack of pushiness instilled trust in the female customers. A few times she even was reprimanded by her boss for discouraging a customer from buying a car that Jen knew they couldn't afford and convincing them to settle for a lesser model. She enjoyed her job and was very good at doing it, and her sales commissions grew as repeat customers would often ask for her.

Dave had added a new side venture of his own. Having been issued a federal firearms license, he began buying and selling guns. The profit was nice, of course, but holding and using those various guns was just plain fun for Dave. After a year or so of that, another opportunity arose and Dave traded in one of his more expensive handguns for a set of premium stainless steel cookware that he and Jen eventually sold through home demonstrations. They found themselves doing very well in the cookware business as well, recording record sales their first year and winning a prize trip to Westbend, Wisconsin.

But despite their efforts, climbing out of their pit of debt was a long, arduous effort. More money was coming in but paying off all of those credit cards, even with a lot of discipline, was tough. So when Jen was offered the opportunity to follow her boss to another sales job in Columbus, Indiana, at the large prestigious BMW dealership that he would be managing there, she and Dave decided to go for it.

After eight years at Magna, Dave had pretty much climbed the company ladder as far as he could go, and was making way too much money for his own good. He'd begun running CNC (computer numeric controlled) lathes the past few years, giving him very marketable experience for his young age. Knowing there were machine shops everywhere and with his skill set and experience he'd be able to get a job, Dave had left Magna and followed Jen to Columbus in the fall of 1985.

Not only were the job opportunities enticing, but they agreed it would be good for their young family to get away for a while, away from their partying friends, away from temptations that had become bad habits, away from the familiar and toward a fresh start. The financial situation had put undue stress on their marriage, and perhaps this was the new beginning they both needed.

And so the young couple, with eighteen-month-old Chris in tow, packed up their belongings and moved 90 minutes away to the southern Indiana city of Columbus. Jen slid easily into her new job selling luxury vehicles while Dave's machining experience opened many job opportunities for him, eventually settling into a well-paid position with Star Tool. Over the next six years, Dave honed his valuable CNC skills and eventually was trained as an EDM (electrical discharge machine) machinist, a very specialized and new skill set at that time. While working 60 hours a week including holidays at an already-good base salary gave Dave lots of overtime pay, it didn't leave much family time.

But despite the long work weeks, Dave somehow always made time to have fun with his work buddies. Too much fun. During work breaks they would flip coins for money or even paychecks, gambling, and playing cards. Most evenings after work found the small group of friends drinking in a nearby bar. Sundays were spent, not in church with their respective families, but golfing together.

Thankfully, Jen's work schedule was very flexible and she was able to rearrange her schedule as needed. While Jen was selling cars and Dave was machining tools, Chris spent his toddler days at KinderCare. After a couple of years in Columbus, Jen became involved at the Burnsville Christian Church, an outlet for her musical talents as well as the much-needed roots of a church family that she had missed. So while Dave and his buddies golfed away most Sunday mornings, Jen took Chris to church.

Dave's drinking and partying simply annoyed Jen at first, but she became increasingly frustrated as it slowly escalated over the months and years they lived in Columbus. Eventually those after-dinner drinks with his buddies extended into the early morning hours, with Dave often going home for just a few hours then back out at midnight to hang with his friends again until 3 or 4 a.m. Lots of booze and little sleep didn't seem to faze Dave, and there seemed to be no consequences for his wild lifestyle as he continued to be successful at work, and between the two working parents the money kept rolling in.

On January 7, 1990, Nathan Daniel Bell arrived to the delight of his parents. With two precious sons, great careers, and a nice home with plenty of "things," life for Dave and Jen seemed to be just about as good as they could ever hope. The debt weight still hung over them, but slowly they were making progress on that. By all appearances and worldly checklists, they were doing well. But something was missing, something big that neither of them could quite put their finger on.

Harsh realities of life have a way of shaking up people who need a drastic wake-up call. Such was the case with Dave and Jen, when they were stunned by the news that Dave's best friend Mark had been paralyzed from the waist down in a freak diving accident and would spent the rest of his days in a wheelchair. For the first time in his life, Dave was shaken to the core. There really were no guarantees in life, and too often blessings are taken for granted. God had gotten his attention, at least for the moment.

Then not too many months later, Dave received another wake-up call that would literally save his life and his family. Coming home drunk one evening when Nate was not yet a year old, Dave went to pick up his infant son and Nate refused to go to him. Even in his drunken state, Dave didn't miss the terrified look in Nate's eyes, and that picture of his young son's fearful face permanently seared into Dave's mind and crushed him to the very soul of his being. God had his undivided attention. After that incident, Dave would never abuse alcohol again.

It was a life-changing season for Dave and Jen. Although they would spend yet another year in Columbus, they both felt a deep longing to go back home after Dave's father Myron suffered a heart attack. And in the summer of 1991, when Chris was seven years old and Nate eighteen months, the Bells moved back home to the Hagerstown area.

Finding an old farmhouse on Indiana 38 available to rent, Dave and Jen settled in with their young family. The country home was midway between both of their families' homes and in a nice location, nestled under some big shade trees with plenty of yard for their boys. The house was old and worn and had been uninhabited for several years, but it was structurally sound, and the owner was grateful for the young couple's willingness to fix it up, gradually making it livable again.

Connections Dave had at Star opened a welcome door of opportunity to run a new machine shop, Academy Wire Services, in Knightstown. This shop had the only EDM machine in the area and Dave's unique EDM skills made him the perfect choice to operate the shop for the out-of-town owner, most weeks working 80 hours or more. Often Dave would take his young sons to spend days at the shop with him, when Chris was out of school for the summer and Nate was just a toddler. Meanwhile, Jen decided to change her career path and began training to become a Certified Nursing Assistant, initially working the night shift at a Middletown nursing home and later doing home health care through Reid Hospital in Richmond.

Desiring to continue her growing faith, Jen began once more attending White Branch Church of the Brethren with her two young boys. Even though White Branch was the church in which Dave had grown up, his attendance was hit-and-miss for a while. But after listening to Chris continually asking him why he wasn't going to church with them, Dave's heart softened and he also began attending regularly with Jen. And in the fall of 1992, at the invitation of her mother-in-law Phyllis, Jen enrolled in Bible Study Fellowship, taking Nate to the children's classes that coincided with the women's studies.

As Dave and Jen slowly became involved in White Branch Church, they reunited with a couple that Dave had known through his childhood Brethren Church camp experiences. The Shivelys were retiring from their position as Brethren District Youth Advisors, and wondered if Dave and Jen might consider taking over that role. And so it happened that soon the Bells accepted the volunteer position, becoming youth advisors overseeing events and conferences for 74 Brethren church youth groups. In their very limited free time, Dave and Jen worked with and came to know many wonderful Christian teens in their district, a ministry opportunity they greatly enjoyed.

Believing they had finally found their happy niche in life, Dave and Jen approached the owner of their rental home and property about possibly purchasing it. The owner, a retired brain surgeon-turned-university professor who lived in another state, was eager to get rid of the property and gave the Bells a great deal. They bought the house and eleven acres for $30,000, and even talked the owner into applying the past two years of rent they had paid onto the mortgage. It was then that their dream of owning their own wire-machining business, Cutting Edge, began to take shape.

Starting a new business was a daunting proposition. First came the zoning problems, when the neighbors protested the idea of having a business disrupt their quiet, peaceful country life. Eventually the Bells were able to get the necessary approval of the authorities to move ahead and calm the unfounded fears of the neighbors, but it wasn't easy. Then, still heavily in personal debt, came the question of where they would get the seed money to start Cutting Edge.

God knew the answer. In the spring of 1994, a wayward spark from a trash fire landed on an old out-building next to the Bells' big barn causing a three-alarm fire that destroyed the barn and everything the family had stored inside it as well as damaging their home. Dave, with the help of his dad Myron, had been cleaning out and tearing down some of the dilapidated structures on the property, burning the old wood and trash in a big fire. In a rash action that Dave would later describe as "stupidity," he heaved an ancient five-pound rusted can of gunpowder onto the trash fire. He'd barely had time to turn around and begin walking away when the earth-shattering explosion knocked Dave to the ground and sent showers of sparks flying! In what could have been a catastrophe, no one was injured and the scattered sparks were put out. Or so they thought, until hours later, when they discovered that their barn was being consumed by fire.

The insurance money from that huge fire along with a generous loan from a good friend provided the money needed to construct the Cutting Edge building on the back part of their property and purchase the first EDM machine. By fall of 1994, Cutting Edge was officially in business. Once more, Dave realized that God had been preparing him for this season of his life. All of the contacts, training, experience, and managerial duties he'd acquired over the past fourteen years became critical elements in getting Cutting Edge off to a running start.

Everything had fallen into place and life was good for the Bells. Jen was working as a CNA as well as serving as Class Administrator for Bible Study Fellowship. It was through BSF that Jen first learned about an African ministry called "Rafiki," an off-shoot ministry of BSF International. Enthralled by her first exposure to Rafiki through the photos she saw and the stories she heard, Jen shared her enthusiasm and confusion with Dave that evening around the supper table. As touched as she was by the eagerness of these people on the other side of the world to hear the gospel, the lack of passion Jen saw in most of the people around her was puzzling. While others were less eager, Jen was a sponge, soaking up all the Bible knowledge she could and growing in her faith and love for Jesus.

At Jen's encouragement, the couple had each signed up to attend back-to-back retreat weekends, The Brethren Way of Christ, in the spring of 1995. Having heard wonderful reviews from their district church friends who had attended, they both knew they would benefit greatly both individually and as a couple from the three-day spiritual pilgrimage weekend. The men's weekend was first, and Dave returned with a changed heart and a totally new outlook on life.

So new, in fact, that Jen became a little leery about attending the women's weekend herself. When Dave came to bed later that evening after returning home from the retreat, he carried his Bible and began reading it in bed. Jen didn't say anything, but he had definitely gotten her attention! The next day he prayed before their family meals, and each day that week Dave brought Jen a card and small gift. Who was this man? And what had happened to her husband??? While she certainly appreciated the extra attention and new behaviors, Jen became apprehensive herself about how the coming weekend might change her as well. She'd tried asking Dave about the weekend's details, but all he could say was he was so glad he went and couldn't wait for her to go as well.

Following Jen's own personal revival that following weekend, her craving for a stronger relationship with God was deepened. That shared experience was a spiritual awakening for both of them individually, as well as a couple. They were sold out to Jesus, separate from the world, and hungry for more. While Dave had dealt with his own falling away from God, Jen also had her own issues with which to come to terms. She began turning over her struggles to God…her tendency toward financial hoarding, her resistance to gift-giving, and her desire for perfectionism, all of which were roadblocks that hindered her complete surrender to God's will for her life.

Together they chose the Bible passage that would become their life verses, the one they would build their future upon and refer back to when life got rough and the road uncertain. *"Trust in the Lord with all your heart and lean not on your own understanding; in all your ways acknowledge Him, and He will make your paths straight."* (Proverbs 3: 5-6, NIV). They memorized the verse and recited it often, and Dave even had it painted on the tailgate of his business truck.

Their Brethren Way weekend also lit another fire; the youth they worked with needed something similar to ignite their faith. Through connections with some mutual friends, they learned about similar retreats for teens through other denominations and decided to create a youth weekend they would call Faith Quest for Brethren youth in their district.

And so, working with a few pastors and close friends, God directed as Dave and Jen put together Faith Quest. It was a huge multi-faceted endeavor, a task that might have seemed too big had God not been authoring it. In just six months, they organized and wrote the entire thing, with Dave and Jen personally penning eight of the fourteen talks given during the weekend. It took a lot of passionate convincing for the Church of the Brethren to give the new program its blessing, but the Bells led their first Faith Quest in 1995. The twice-a-year retreat would continue long past Dave and Jen's four-year involvement, and over the next twenty years they would continue to be amazed at the ripples that continue from that initial dream and desire God put into their hearts to begin Faith Quest.

The years of 1995-1996 proved to be a period of tremendous spiritual growth for the Bells. During an eighteen-month span, they prayerfully left White Branch Church and began worshiping at Anderson Church of the Brethren. Besides the huge task of beginning Faith Quest, they also had the blessing of attending Dennis and Barbara Rainey's family life/marriage retreat as well as sitting under the financial teaching of Larry Burkett to become trained financial counselors. God was opening many doors through which they were eagerly walking, taking advantage of opportunities and learning to live out Biblical principles in all aspects of their lives.

In 1996, Dave also began attending Bible Study Fellowship, taking young Chris for the evening children's program and soon serving as a children's leader himself. Dave had become very involved in the local Little League organization, taking on the role of league vice-president and with Jen's help shouldering the large summer task of running the concession stand. By all appearances, they were a normal American family, very busy and involved in their community. But deep down a nagging dissatisfaction persisted. They were "living the dream," but it wasn't satisfying.

A big move came in 1996, when the Bells decided to forego the traditional American Christmas celebration. No decorations, no tree, no presents. Instead of exchanging gifts, the family enjoyed a two-week Florida vacation to escape the holiday madness, spending Christmas Day together serving meals to the homeless at the Sarasota Salvation Army. The family values were shifting, slowly but surely, as Dave and Jen desperately sought to teach their children to live out Christian principles as best they knew how.

While service was on their minds and hearts, the realities of their financial responsibilities still loomed large. Chipping away at the mountain of debt was a painfully slow process, but they began to see a dim light at the end of the long tunnel. They set a goal to be debt-free by the turn of the millennium. And month by month, bill by bill, they worked toward complete financial freedom that the year 2000 would bring.

Patiently, steadily, licking and turning.

CHAPTER 6

Sold Out to Jesus

June 2000

D ave started the truck and looked up into the rearview mirror. Everything they owned was tucked beneath those straps in the truck bed...a few family heirloom furniture pieces that Jen had inherited from her grandparents, keepsake boxes of the boys' baby pictures and memorabilia, a hope chest Dave had given to Jen years ago, dishes and a few basic kitchen supplies, and a couple of suitcases of clothing. All their worldly belongings, every earthly possession, packed into the back of that black and silver Dodge Ram.

He didn't look back, but instead turned his head toward Jen and smiled. At that moment, pulling out onto State Road 38 and away from everything he'd ever known, Dave felt happier and freer than he'd ever felt in his entire life.

Just three months before, Dave and Jen had signed the final sale documents and turned their successful business Cutting Edge Wire EDM over to Steve Cross, the new owner. Once the decision was made, the couple did not look back. God was leading them a whole new direction, one they had never in their wildest dreams anticipated.

It's hard to say exactly when that first seed was planted, but in retrospect Dave and Jen could see that God's hand had been at work for years prior to this day. Perhaps it had been planted that very day that Dave and Jen joined their lives together in matrimony. Perhaps it had been that eye-opening 1995 retreat where Dave insisted he'd never go to Africa, or perhaps Jen's exposure to Rafiki at BSF perked up their ears to God's insistent calling. But there was no doubt that the seed was lovingly nurtured in the fall of 1998, when both Dave and Jen studied the book of Genesis through Bible Study Fellowship.

The Biblical account of Abraham's call hit them both separately and simultaneously. Reading and studying those familiar chapters in Genesis suddenly took on an all-new, extremely personal meaning. God had called Abraham, seemingly out-of-the-blue, to leave his country and his people and the only life he'd ever known to go where God would lead. And Abraham obeyed. Without hesitation, without knowing where he was going or what he would do when he got there, Abraham obeyed God's call.

Suddenly, the vision of their future became crystal clear, and not clear at all! Dave and Jen both knew in their hearts that God was also calling them to do exactly that, to leave their comfortable lives and follow Him into unknown territory. To trust and obey. Over the next couple of years, thousands of prayers and dozens of heartfelt discussions would ensue and solidify their belief that God was indeed preparing to lead them out too, much as He'd led Abraham so many thousands of years before.

Following this revelation and new-found purpose and direction, Dave and Jen became even more focused and determined in their preparation to obeying God's call. Cutting Edge was growing by leaps and bounds, and Dave was able to obtain state-of-the-art machinery that literally kept his business on the cutting edge of technology. The business thrived and Dave worked late hours just trying to keep ahead of the mounting orders. Spurred on by their goal of heading into the new millennium financially free and able to follow God's calling unhindered, one by one they paid off their debts, first their personal credit cards and then their business loans. And by November 1999, just in time to meet their self-imposed deadline, Dave and Jen celebrated the amazing feeling of being debt-free for the first time in their seventeen years of marriage.

In August of 1999, the Bells had gotten their first taste of international mission work when they spent a short stint in Mexico with "Companeros en Ministerio," a Tijuana-based ministry partnering with the Church of the Brethren. That week in Mexico was both energizing and eye-opening as the couple ministered to the poorest of the poor in some of the worst slums in the world, built atop a landfill in Tijuana. Culture-shocked by the desperation of these people so hungry for love and the gospel, the Bells felt like they were on another planet worlds away from the familiar cornfields of Indiana. Poverty took on a whole new level of meaning there in that dump when the Bells witnessed the desperate hunger of a young boy, ripping the top off an old, dirty container of cottage cheese and gobbling up the putrid contents as he watched them walk by, definitely a reality check for the green missionaries. Yet in the midst of all the suffering, for the first time in a very long time they experienced the deep satisfaction of sacrificing self for the Kingdom, and they both knew they'd hit a chord that resonated deeply within them. Perhaps this was exactly where God was leading them to serve!

So they returned to Indiana more resolute than ever, eager to do whatever it took to live that life of deep-soul satisfaction that only comes from heeding God's call, and joyfully finished paying off their final debts. The following spring of 2000 they brought their sons Chris (who was fifteen years old) and Nate (nine years old) along with them and returned to Mexico with three different mission teams, working alongside the Companeros team leaders. Flying into Los Angeles, they would spend a day or two handing out food and praying with homeless drug addicts on the streets of LA's skid row. The filth and deplorable conditions were shocking, a horde of seemingly forgotten humankind ducking in and out of cardboard-box shelters, shooting up on the sidewalks, defecating in the streets. The putrid smell of wasting humanity hovered unseen, the invisible sense of hopeless desperation permeating their nostrils. Gang culture governed those streets, and more than once Dave and Jen felt a real sense of fear for their lives and the lives of their boys. But despite the uneasiness, they never doubted God's presence with them as they served. After a day or two in LA, they would drive to Tijuana, Mexico, smuggling in building and ministry supplies to work in the slum cities built atop the dumps and landfills.

Chris and Nate were definitely getting an alternative educational experience! When they had decided to give their lives to full-time mission work, Dave and Jen had begun home-schooling their two boys to enable them to travel unencumbered by a school schedule. Serving alongside their parents, those experiences etched an indelible compassion for the less fortunate that would play out in their adult lives years later.

Following those short-term stints in Mexico, the Bells found themselves even more passionate about sharing the gospel to the unsaved, learning and applying new life lessons about how to prepare, teach, and especially trust in the Lord. And in a whirlwind of determination and newfound direction, they prayed about implementing a plan for Cutting Edge that would free them to seek God's will unhindered.

The logical thing to do, Dave and Jen decided, was to hire someone who could manage the business so they could travel abroad as the need arose. When they proposed a well-thought-out arrangement with a trusted and skilled acquaintance, he showed no interest in running the shop for them. Clearly disappointed, Dave walked back to the house to share with Jen the news of the refused proposal. Jen, who had been praying for God's will that whole afternoon, told Dave that she felt God wanted them to sell the business.

Sell Cutting Edge? After all the blood, sweat, and tears that had gone into making it the success it was just now showing? It seemed ridiculous. Couldn't they do so much more for the Kingdom if they kept the business and used the profits for ministry? Wasn't that the best business plan for God?

God quickly showed them that His plan trumped their best human ideas when the phone rang the following morning with a purchase offer from the gentleman who had turned down their management proposal the previous day. He wanted to buy Cutting Edge, if they were willing to sell.

The pieces were falling into place. But the Bells had no idea what would be a fair selling price for the business. How much was it worth? Besides the concrete value of equipment and materials on hand, they had no idea how much Cutting Edge was actually worth as a business entity. They researched and hashed it over and over, but just couldn't come up with a monetary value. So they decided to diligently pray, each of them separately, that God would give them a fair asking price. After a time of prayer, both Dave and Jen each independently wrote down the number that they felt God had given them and were absolutely astonished that both came up with exactly the same price! It was, without a doubt, definitely a God-thing. And when they shared their God-given selling price with the prospective buyer, he accepted on the spot without even a counter offer.

Shortly after the sale of Cutting Edge, a very similar scenario played out once more when the Bells received an out-of-the-blue phone call from someone interested in buying their home. Having heard about the sale of the business, a young woman who had grown up nearby wondered if they might be interested in selling their house to her so she could be close to her parents. Dave and Jen really hadn't thought about selling their home at that time, thinking instead they would hang onto it so they would have a home base between mission trips abroad. But they prayed about it and once more asked God to give them a fair selling price. It had worked once before, so they decided to try it again. And once more, God impressed upon both Dave and Jen separately a matching selling price which was, once again, accepted without counter. Amazed, yet beginning to learn not to be surprised, the Bells would say that when God is your real estate agent you've got nothing to worry about.

In March of 2000, Dave and Jen signed away Cutting Edge to a brand new owner. And a few short months later, in the summer of 2000 while they were away for an eleven-week stint in Mexico, the final paperwork on the sale of their home was finalized. The strings that had held them had been severed.

Not surprisingly, everyone around them thought they had lost their minds. Dave's family, who had always been very close-knit, especially struggled to understand. Why would they feel the need to leave their successful life for an as-yet-unspecified ministry abroad? Couldn't they use their many resources here to spread the gospel just as effectively? The questions were many, and Dave and Jen didn't seem to have any particularly satisfying answers except that they were being obedient to God's calling. While they were totally at peace and knew they were in God's will, no one else quite seemed to get it. Hardest to leave behind would be their aging parents. Dave had the assurance that Phyllis had always prayed for her children to be in the center of God's will. Even if that meant they would be in another country and far, far, far away from home.

Just where God was leading them, they had no clear knowledge. But neither had Abraham and Sarah when they too had packed up and left for worlds unknown. Dave and Jen had each other, their adolescent sons (Chris now sixteen years old and Nate ten years), and God's undeniable call. It was all they needed.

And so it was, on that sunny day in June 2000, Dave reached across the seat and gave Jen's hand a squeeze as they pulled out of the driveway for what would be the final time. He turned the truck west, heading the few miles to his parents' home where they would unload the few belongings they had, storing them and the truck in the elder Bells' barn. With some of the profits from the sale of Cutting Edge, they bought a van, packed a few sets of clothing, and a couple of days later hit the road toward California.

Homeless. Jobless. And even churchless, for it was also at this time that with much angst and sadness the Bells left their Anderson

Church of the Brethren family amidst the controversial hiring of a new liberal-thinking pastor whose theology was worlds away from Dave and Jen's Biblical views. The Bells were in searching mode, waiting and trusting that God would lead them where He wanted them to serve.

Having been bitten hard by the missionary bug while working with Companeros the year before, it seemed only logical that God was sending them to LA and Mexico to do more ministry in the slums of Tijuana and the Baja Peninsula. Buoyed by the excitement of the adventure that surely lay ahead, the family made a vacation of their trip west, stopping at the Grand Canyon and other landmarks along the way. Over the years, Chris and Nate would never let their dad forget the time he proudly pointed out a dead armadillo along the side of a Texas road, only to have to sheepishly admit that it was actually just a piece of old rubber instead! Eventually they arrived at skid row in East LA, their presumed home base for their mission work ahead, and jumped headlong and heart-strong into their new passion. They could see themselves spending long months there, organizing building projects and leading short-term teams into Tijuana.

Working hard all day and falling into bed exhausted each night, the Bells were nonetheless exhilarated by their new mission. They had already made plans to homeschool their sons, so as the summer weeks rolled by they soon settled into a new routine. While they were in Mexico, they received word that their home sale was finalized. Now they truly were homeless, yet freer than they had ever felt. Over suppers Dave and Jen dreamed of long-term mission work there, even contemplated purchasing a 28-room hotel in Tijuana to use for the ministry. Ever the planner and strategist, Dave envisioned the two of them filling the role of eventually running the Companeros ministry in Mexico. He could barely sleep at night, his mind ruminating with visions and plans to put into place in the coming months, maybe even years.

Eleven weeks after they arrived, the Bells' mission work in Mexico came to a screeching halt. It was a lesson Dave and Jen would learn over and over again: God's plans were often not the same as theirs. When the leadership position of the Companeros ministry by-passed them and went into other missionaries' hands, they found themselves floundering in uncertainty once again. They packed up their meager belongings, bid farewell to their friends, donated their van to Companeros, and boarded a plane for Indiana.

During those eleven weeks, Dave and Jen had certainly been diligently praying and contemplating where God would next lead them. While they thought a long-term mission stint in Mexico was a distinct possibility, they were also open to other mission destinations. When a planned trip to Cuba through their Companeros connections fell through, followed by the disappointment of a long-term Mexico ministry with Companeros also falling through, they were approached about a trip to Vietnam with another young couple and so the planning began for that.

With their house sold and their future in God's hands, Dave and Jen were thankful for the welcome open doors of Phyllis and Myron's home where they stayed between mission trips. While moving back in with his folks was not easy for any of them, everyone was grateful for this extra time together and especially the bonding opportunities Chris and Nate had with their Bell grandparents. Knowing that eventually they would not be living locally, it was a welcome respite for Dave and Jen to stay with Phyllis and Myron and be close to Jen's parents for this short season of their lives.

Just before going to Mexico for those eleven weeks that they'd hoped would turn into months or perhaps even years of ministry with Companeros, in July 2000 Dave and Jen, at the invitation of friends, traveled to Wisconsin to volunteer for Lifest, a week-long Christian youth event sponsored by Life Promotions. Little did they realize at the time, Life Promotions would soon become a big part of their lives. But before leading them to Wisconsin to work with Life Promotions, God had a few more life-changing international experiences in store for them.

Vietnam was one of those. Chomping at the bit to serve but not quite sure yet where God was leading them, when the opportunity arose for a short-term mission trip to Vietnam, Dave and Jen jumped at the chance to explore new mission possibilities as well as expose their family to another very different culture. So in November 2000, traveling with another family from Tabor Baptist Church, their new church home, Dave, Jen, Chris, and Nate flew into Saigon. The goal for the one-month venture was to smuggle in and distribute Bibles and do teaching in Vietnam's underground church, a very dangerous proposition yet one the Bells and their friends were eager to undertake, an opportunity to share the gospel with people literally starving for truth and hope.

And light. THE LIGHT of the world! The dark culture they experienced in Vietnam was very different from anything the young missionaries had ever felt, a palpable poverty of spirit as well as physical poverty, weighted down by a seemingly impenetrable tradition of ancestral worship where giving one's life to Jesus meant forsaking all family ties and could even cost one's own life. Christianity in Vietnam was not for the faint of heart, but it was also that very hunger for truth that led people to literally risk their very lives for their belief in Jesus. Invigorating, terrifying, exhilarating, exasperating, definitely a new challenge for these young missionaries with limited experience.

Following the 24-hour trip from the other side of the world, Dave and Jen and their boys exhaustedly fell into their Saigon hotel beds around midnight and barely got to sleep when they were awakened in the early predawn hours by a phone call from their hostess/leader/translator/guide Bao. "Prepare for a visitor quickly" was her brief hurried message to them. Moments later, Dave opened the door to a tiny, bent-over old man, his dirty rags of clothing not able to hide the ravages of an obviously hard life. Bones protruded through dry crinkled skin as he quietly hobbled into the room as quickly as his crippled legs allowed. But his dark, sunken eyes lit up, illuminating his entire countenance, when Dave opened a suitcase and those eyes fell upon the stack of Bibles inside. It was the first of many moments when the Bells discovered that God's Word and love overcame language barriers, as the ancient man profusely thanked them, speaking not a word of English yet both parties completely understood. And then, as quickly as he had appeared, he shuffled out the door carrying as many Bibles as his scrawny yet strong arms could manage.

The early morning encounter seemed surreal, and seemed even more so when Bao told them the rest of the story. This old man was a pastor and had just been released from prison the day before, having been arrested five years ago for sharing the Gospel. Prison life was not kind to him, and during those five long years he had been repeatedly abused and severely beaten. Yet less than 24 hours after being released, instead of laying low and enjoying his freedom, he was clamoring for Bibles to begin sharing the Gospel yet again. This was a picture of faith that the Bells had not yet experienced first-hand, people so hungry for God that they were willing and even eager to put themselves in danger to spread His Word.

Vietnam would prove to provide lots of "firsts" for the Bells. For the first time, Dave and Jen were sharing the Gospel in extreme situations, sneaking into homes at night for secret worship. Carrying contraband Bibles that, if discovered, would have landed them in prison at the very least with much more severe earthly consequences at the worst. Being constantly shadowed by government vehicles wherever they went. Having the emails they sent home from a Saigon cyber café being intercepted and never making it out of the country. Sharing the gospel with such diverse groups of people in home worship services that Dave's message in English had to be translated, phrase by phrase, as many as seven times into seven different dialects with Dave often struggling to remember what he had said and just where he was in the gospel story. Running a youth event in a public park surrounded by designated human look-outs, ready to scatter at a moment's warning.

Spurred on by their passion for youth and children, the Bells also spent time working in a children's home staffed by Roman

Catholic nuns. The home was filled with orphaned children as well as older teens, many of them lighter-skinned and suffering from a wide variety of illnesses and physical deformities caused by, according to the nuns they talked with, exposure to Agent Orange left behind by the American military. War is ugly and no doubt atrocities were committed on both sides, but these innocent victims who were some of the Vietnam War's biggest casualties pulled at the heartstrings of Dave and Jen in a special way.

Despite their physical disabilities and seemingly hopeless earthly situation, Jesus shone brightly in the lives of many of those "forgotten" children, forgotten by the world but every-so-precious to God. The nuns, despite their reputation for strict adherence to government standards about what could be said and taught in this "closed" country, had clearly defied the rules and had been teaching the gospel as there were many believers among those young souls. Obviously thrilled to have the Bells' encouragement, the smiling nun who was in charge of the home began showing them around, pulling Dave and Jen aside and whispering to them, "I am Catholic but I know Jesus! I'm so glad He brought you here!"

During the latter part of their month in Vietnam, Dave and Jen and their missionary companions traveled upcountry into Vietnam's Demilitarized Zone. While danger lurked in the dark corners around Saigon, it was a palpable presence in the DMZ. Even travel there was fraught with peril, as they were never given their final destination and driven to seven temporary stopping points, each time getting their next set of directions. They found themselves in the vicinity of Caipai, hiking off-road a mile or more through dense jungle to a remote village where they were welcomed with a jubilant celebration, the villagers killing a chicken and climbing palm trees for fresh coconut to honor their guests. Uneasiness was quickly replaced with delight, the missionary group humbled by the lavish reception. In that village they taught the gospel and planted a church, and the last they heard, that church in the jungle wilds of Vietnam was still growing strong and on fire for the Lord.

Eye-opening, heart-breaking, faith-inspiring…the Vietnam experience was definitely a break-through in the Bells' missionary experience. Seeing such spiritual darkness and hunger for the light and truth just reinforced the urgency they felt to reach more people with the gospel's life-saving message. So many desperately lost people, so little time. Dave was often reminded of his father's simple yet wise childhood advice, so applicable in his new missionary life. Keep moving toward God's goodness, no time to ponder or stand still lest you waste a delicious morsel of blessing. Just lick and turn.

CHAPTER 7

First Taste of Africa

February 2001

Ghana. Zimbabwe.

Ghana? Zimbabwe? Countries on the African continent?!

Poring over the world map spread out before him, Dave's mind did a quick flashback to that day, not so long past yet seemingly lifetimes ago, when he had definitively stated he'd go anywhere God sent him. Anywhere, that is, except Africa. And yet now he stood, Jen at his side, studying the map and wracking his brain for any information he could glean about Ghana and Zimbabwe. Revolutions, famines, genocides, corruption, civil war—it seemed these were the topics of most news stories coming out of Africa. God only knew what He was sending them into...

Zimbabwe was presently the home of missionary friends David and Debbie Lively, where Debbie was the teacher of a Bible Study Fellowship International class and David was a director of the Rafiki ministry. Jen's heartstrings for Africa had first been tugged a few years before by stories the Livelys shared about their Rafiki experiences in Zimbabwe. Coupling that with a loose missionary connection to Ghana through their newfound friend Bob Lenz, who was a well-known national speaker focusing on youth and the founder of the Christian youth organization Life Promotions, based in Wisconsin, Dave and Jen found themselves being led by God across the globe to deep, dark, mysterious Africa. The very place Dave so adamantly swore he would never go.

After returning from their eye-opening month in Vietnam, the Bells fell into the opportunity to purchase a home in Chesterfield, Indiana for a very cheap price. Thinking it would be nice to have a home base from which to operate and not wanting to wear out their welcome constantly boomeranging back to Dave's parents' home, it seemed prudent to have a place to land between mission callings. Chris and Nate worked alongside Dave remodeling the fixer-upper when they had time, and it became home for the Bells whenever they were stateside. When the opportunity arose to minister in Ghana and Zimbabwe, Dave and Jen, with memories of Vietnam still very fresh in their minds and recent unnerving news of Mugabe killings coming out of Zimbabwe, decided to leave the boys behind with family in the US for this first-time venture into as-yet-uncharted waters.

And so it was with excitement mixed with a little healthy trepidation that Dave and Jen began making preparations for their first trip to Africa. They would be working with the Rafiki Foundation, first visiting the Livelys in Zimbabwe and then spending two weeks in Ghana helping start the construction of a new Rafiki children's center there.

As part of their preparation to go, Dave and Jen were invited to meet with Rosemary Jensen, the founder of the Rafiki Foundation and then Executive Director of Bible Study Fellowship International. Since Dave and Jen were both in local BSF leadership roles, they well knew about Ms. Jensen's commitment to Africa. Before her climb to the top of the BSF ladder, Rosemary had been a missionary in Tanzania and it was then God ignited a passion in her to reach the African people with the gospel. During her tenure as BSF Executive Director, Ms. Jensen started the Rafiki Foundation, with the goals of caring for and educating orphans and providing economic opportunities to widows in Africa.

Dave and Jen flew to Rosemary's San Antonio home where she met with them at great length, trying to convince them to become Rafiki missionaries themselves. While they wholeheartedly supported the mission of Rafiki, after much prayer Dave and Jen did not feel that God wanted to limit them only to working through Rafiki. He had placed other ministry ideas on their hearts and minds, and they weren't ready to commit themselves exclusively to Rafiki. But they were eager to see what God was doing through the Rafiki ministry, and Ms. Jensen's insight and knowledge was very valuable in helping them know what to expect.

Arriving in Zimbabwe on February 11, 2001, they were met and hosted by David and Debbie Lively who were serving with Rafiki, working with others attempting to develop the first Rafiki children's villages in Zimbabwe. Having lived in Africa for some time, the Livelys were delighted to open their hearts and home to the Bells and able to share with them first-hand knowledge and encouragement about missionary life. The poverty and hunger Dave and Jen saw in Zimbabwe stunned them, and Jen's heart broke for the children, so many of them orphaned due to the rampant AIDS epidemic that was literally killing off a generation of Africans. The need was astonishing, and Rafiki was a small yet powerful light in a sea of darkness.

Dave and Debbie Lively were also leading men's and women's BSF classes in Harare, the capital city of Zimbabwe, so the Bells were thrilled to experience BSF in another culture, amazed that the same lesson their friends were studying halfway across the world in their lavish homes and comfortable churches in the States was also being studied in the doga huts, crude structures made of mud with thatched roofs, and on hard, rocky ground under the palm trees. Many of the wealthy elite and diplomats of Zimbabwe sat next to the poorest of Zimbabwe Christians in their discussion groups, all equal children of God in His Kingdom. Same truth, same gospel, same love of God for His children no matter their circumstances.

Also on their agenda for the Zimbabwe trip was to test the waters for a possible return trip with Life Promotions. Before they left the US, Life Promotions founder Bob Lenz had given Dave the names and contact information for a couple of pastors and asked him to connect with them if possible while in Zimbabwe. The Bells did indeed get a chance to spend time with the pastor from Mutoko that Bob had recommended.

It was through this pastor that, unfortunately, Dave and Jen also learned a valuable lesson about living in Africa. The black market is rampant and the corrupt nature of folks is the norm. Due to the political unrest, the Bells had been told that there was a fuel shortage and that gasoline was expensive. While that may have been true, the Bells were also naïve and trustingly gave the pastor $50 to buy fuel for his vehicle. That $50 apparently "bought" them less than two gallons. Dave suspects that most of that $50 went into the pastor's pocket. It was another lesson they would learn over and over again: not all countries share the same societal values as Americans. Sadly, government-sanctioned corruption leads to individual corruption in many third world countries, and Zimbabwe was no exception.

So much need in Zimbabwe, it was overwhelming! During their stay, Dave and Jen were able to visit both a leper colony as well as an orphanage in the Mutoko area. With the average lifespan of a Zimbabwean only 43 years, with one out of every five adults being HIV-positive, the urgency for education and the gospel was obvious. Dave and Jen both struggled with feelings of helplessness as just how to best help these people. For their short visit there, God graciously provided them a peace of mind and opportunities to share God's love with the local people.

Dave and Jen also saw the toll AIDS took on the families, not only the obvious physical suffering, but also the mental anguish. Much like their limited encounters with lepers, HIV-positive people and even their families were shunned by the community. Lack of education on how both diseases spread was replaced by fear and superstition, ripping apart families and villages and leaving desperate people even more hopeless. While the AIDS scourge was certainly frightening, Dave and Jen broke down many invisible walls as villagers watched in awe the Bells showing no reluctance or hesitation in ministering to those forgotten by their own society. Even the Bells found themselves amazed at how the love of God transcends even the strongest man-made barriers.

One of their most horrific experiences ever came in Zimbabwe, when they spent several hours in a government mental hospital. Anyone who did not fit their society's definition of "normal" was institutionalized in hospitals such as these. "Hospital" was a term loosely-used here, as the lack of care was abominable and nearly unbearable to witness. The noise, smells, sounds, and overall hopelessness just blew away the Bells. Seeing some patients who didn't seem to have obvious physical or mental issues, Dave and Jen talked to them and discovered that the government had no other place to put them, so this hospital became their prison for life.

So much despair, so much need, so much darkness. And yet, in the midst of the hopelessness, God was using the Livelys to bring hope, care, and light to those few orphans and widows with whom they came in contact. Rafiki was obviously a bright light to those lives, and Dave and Jen left Zimbabwe convicted to somehow, some way be able to share the gospel amongst some of the poorest people on the earth.

Before they left, the Livelys concocted a surprise for Dave -- a surprise safari from the bed of a pick-up truck! Under the pretense of visiting a neighbor who lived on a "small" ranch of several thousand acres, Dave Bell had his first-ever safari, a private affair with his own tour guide, where he saw his first giraffe and elephant and zebra and all sorts of African wildlife, an unforgettable and awesome experience. Trevor had lived there with his family for over twenty years, the second generation on this family ranch. Dave would learn after returning home that sometime later, President Mugabe's soldiers invaded the ranch, beat Trevor's guards and many of his farm hands, and kicked his family off their family farm. The Bells had literally barely dodged that bullet.

Following their mind-boggling experience in Zimbabwe, Dave and Jen traveled to Accra, Ghana for a two-week stint, again with Rafiki, where they stayed with Rafiki staff and their families who graciously opened their homes and exhibited great hospitality and love to their fellow Christian workers. Among the most vivid memories Dave and Jen took home from their time in Ghana was the nearly unbearable extreme heat and constant exhaustion. Jen, who is normally cold-natured, declared she was hot for the first time in her life. Scorching, searing, BURNING HOT!!!

Jen spent her days at a local Osu Orphanage, working with some of the children that would soon move to the new Rafiki children's center when it was completed. It was her first time dealing with HIV orphans, and she gained invaluable experience that would prove to serve her well in coming years.

While Jen was sweating inside the stuffy, airless orphanage, Dave was pouring his own sweat onto the jungle floor. His job was to help build the perimeter fence around the new children's center property, which involved hand-carrying 200-pound fence posts for long distances through the jungle in 120-degree heat, a tough physical challenge even for this work-seasoned farm boy. Sometimes he felt like the frozen Tampico orange juice pouches were the only thing keeping him alive! Never had he experienced such demanding physical labor in such suffocating and exhausting heat.

The Ghana jungle, like most places in the wilds of Africa, is a very dangerous place, and Dave's work mate Abraham gave him a wildlife reality check. Walking back to the truck for yet another fence post, Dave saw a gorgeous iridescent snake slither across the path in front of him. Before Dave even had a chance to speak, Abraham quickly hacked off its bright green head with his machete. Dave commented on Abraham's violent reaction, reminding him what a beautiful creature it was and how all snakes are not necessarily bad, and asked Abraham what kind of snake it was. "A two-step," answered Abraham. Thinking it an odd name, Dave inquired a bit further. "When it bites a man, he has two steps before he is dead." Dave gulped. He was definitely not in Indiana anymore!

After three emotionally, physically, and spiritually exhausting weeks in Africa, Dave and Jen were certainly thankful to fall into their warm, comfortable bed back in Chesterfield, Indiana. Africa had been wonderful and challenging, exhilarating and frustrating, compelling and disheartening. And yet, they both could feel it. Something about Africa gets under one's skin, and God had already placed in their hearts a nagging desire to return someday.

Funny how God so often twists our plans and opinions, if we only let Him. Dave found that out firsthand when God caused him to fall in love with Africa, the very place he dared God to send him. Yet another lesson in obedience, another opportunity to lick and turn.

CHAPTER 8

New Perspectives, Merging Passions

April 2001

A dream? Or a nightmare?! Awakened from his sound sleep by a loud rushing sound and unspeakable stench, Dave jumped out of bed into dark wetness, flipped on lights and followed the rushing sound to the bathroom and the scene of the plumbing disaster.

No, he wasn't in Africa. Or Mexico or LA's skid row. Through his travels, Dave's senses had been assaulted by innumerable disgusting scenarios and stomach-turning smells. But what he experienced at 2:00 a.m. that morning in his newly-remodeled Chesterfield, Indiana home rivaled all of those as he discovered the origin of the horrific mess. Wading through nasty, stinky brown water into the basement bathroom, he discovered the toilet erupting raw sewage everywhere! The toilet lid had been blown off by the blast and had bounced off the wall a couple of feet away, now floating in the rapidly-rising lake of waste.

Dave would find out later that the previous evening's heavy rainfall had been too much for the town's aged sewer system to handle and the pressure of that logjam of waste caused it to explode into the Bells' basement. Since returning from Africa just a couple of months before, Dave and his sons had worked hard renovating the basement, putting in a master bedroom, Nate's bedroom, and a bath. New fixtures, new flooring, new paint, new furniture, all now damaged by several inches of raw sewage.

To add to the calamity, Chris and Nate were both sleeping on the basement floor to accommodate their houseguest for the week. It so happened that Dave's now-good friend Bob Lenz, the founder of Life Promotions, was staying with them for a few days. Bob, along with their mutual friend AJ the Animated Illusionist, had been visiting several area schools, sponsoring student convocations to share the gospel in a fun way with students. Up to their ankles in sewage water, Dave and Jen put the also-soaked boys on their backs to get them to the stairs, handing them things to carry to dry ground.

Up until this plumbing disaster, what a great week it had been! The gospel message had been well-received, with the Bells, Bob, and AJ witnessing many young lives being surrendered to the Lord. God's power was drawing new believers to Himself, and Dave and Jen, who had always had a passion for youth ministry, felt so blessed to be used by Him in this way. The Bells and their friends were witnessing God's glory daily, and apparently Satan got a little jealous and retaliated.

Retaliated by spewing raw sewage. Looking back, Dave and Jen would realize what an appropriate retaliation by the evil one, and yet it did not stop them from carrying on with their scheduled presentation at another school a few hours later. God is so much bigger than a few inches of nasty waste! In an amazing twist to the story, Bob shared the Bells' plight on a radio interview which was heard by the Christian owner of a local professional cleaning company who immediately got to work on the Bell home and rescued them from the mess.

A few years ago, a catastrophe like this would've sent the Bells reeling. But God had brought them so far. After experiencing so many deplorable living conditions in third world countries, this "first world problem" was not nearly as big a deal as it could have been. Amidst the stench, they HAD a flush toilet and a sewer system and the resources to repair and replace material items that really have no eternal value anyway. And through the experience, God had moved in mighty and unexpected ways, turning a terrible situation into a tolerable one through new friendships, new believers, and new insights into His domination over even Satan's best attempts to derail the spreading of the gospel.

God never wastes experiences. Subtly, through their short time as missionaries, He had given the Bells new perspectives on what is valuable and what is not, that this earth is not our home, and our earthly possessions are just things that won't last. People matter, and living for God and sharing the gospel to the world is the only eternal goal worth seeking. God showed them that missions is much more than traveling to a far-off country to share the gospel. There were missions all around them, opportunities for ministry around every corner.

Homeschooling Chris (by now a high school senior) and Nate (doing sixth-grade studies) was a big part of the Bells' family life. Disciplined and organized, Jen took the lead role mapping out this endeavor while sharing the teaching responsibilities with Dave. Two years ago, when Dave and Jen had left behind their American-dream lifestyle to obey God's calling into the mission field, the decision had been made to continue their sons' schooling at home. After much research and prayer, Dave and Jen felt that it would be the best fit for their family, allowing them the freedom and flexibility to travel and minister as God directed. While there were the occasional challenges and frustrations, most of the time the family had a lot of fun homeschooling. Chris would often come to the kitchen table still in his pajamas, pretending to be driving himself to school.

Family prayer times were also very special to the Bells in this season of their lives. Each morning, they would take turns praying for protection and guidance for that day. One infamous prayer time would never be forgotten, and still brings smiles to the Bells' faces when they remember Jen's prayer one morning after a couple of particularly tough days. Intending to ask God to protect them from Satan's fiery darts, her tongue got twisted and she instead asked God to protect them from Satan's diary farts! Needless to say, with two teenage boys in the circle, God surely had a sense of humor as they were unable to finish that prayer time because the whole family was rolling on the floor in hysterical laughter!

Over the next several months, Dave and Jen became more involved in their friend Bob's ministry. While their passion for overseas ministry was still strong and had a powerful pull, bringing youth to know and love the Lord had also always been very dear to their hearts. As they became closer to Bob and through many conversations and vision-casting sessions, it became apparent to all of them that God was calling them to merge these two passions – youth and international mission work – through Life Promotions.

Slowly and steadily, Dave and Jen began helping Bob out with Life Promotions, based in Appleton, Wisconsin, doing necessary behind-the-scenes tasks and filling temporary roles from their Indiana home office. In July 2000, the summer before, they had volunteered at their first Lifest, Life Promotions' biggest outreach event. At that time Lifest was the second-largest Christian youth music festival event in the country, drawing 18,000-20,000 people to Oshkosh, Wisconsin each July.

During this first Lifest experience for the Bells, total strangers had graciously offered the family the entire basement apartment of their very nice home on Lake Winnebago as a living quarters during the event. Although neither of them had any inkling at the time, the hospitality of this couple, Reid and Deana Ribble, would lead to a very valuable friendship for Dave and Jen. Reid would eventually become a US Senator, and God knew Senator Ribble's connections both in Washington, DC and internationally would come in quite handy for the Bells years down the road. Once more, God was orchestrating much bigger plans than any of them could imagine. But for now, it was simply a generous gesture by new acquaintances and a wonderful place for the Bell family to stay on their frequent trips to Wisconsin.

Blown away by the impact of Lifest, since July 2000 the Bells had stayed involved with Life Promotions as much as time allowed. After volunteering in November 2000 at the Power of One event, their son Chris even traveled with Bob Lenz and his team for a short time.

Over the course of several months, as time allowed, Dave and Jen became an integral part of the Life Promotions team. While their actual roles were slowly evolving and not yet clearly defined, Dave and Jen both felt sure that God was directing them to be a part of the organization. The months leading up to Lifest 2001 were busy ones, as the Bells spent countless hours helping prepare: laying out and assigning 2000 campsites, recruiting and managing the 1000+ volunteers, and scheduling and organizing many of the logistics required to make the huge event run smoothly. Exhausting and exhilarating, Lifest 2001 would also be the launching pad for Dave and Jen's brand new ministry -- the Life Promotions Missions Program.

The perfect merger! This new missions program through Life Promotions was announced at Lifest 2001, providing youth a chance to travel across the US and globe to share the gospel and serve others. Dave and Jen would be leading these teams, several each year, to different destinations. Through their mission travels over the past couple of years, God had allowed them to make many international contacts and gain experience to confidently lead youth on life-changing mission trips. God had opened the door for the Bells to do what they knew God had put them on this earth to do -- share the gospel and lead youth to salvation through Christ.

After taking a few deep breaths following an awesome Lifest that year, Dave and Jen began to do some soul-searching on where God wanted them to live. Feeling certain that Life Promotions was their calling at this time in their lives, it sure would be easier if they were in Wisconsin, near the Life Promotions headquarters. While much of their work could be done via phone calls and emails, it was necessary to make many long road trips to meet with people and do on-site planning. But they had also really just gotten settled in Indiana, bought a home, and adding to that was the reality that Jen's mother was fighting cancer and Dave's parents were aging too. The Bells were torn between staying in Indiana for precious time with their families or moving to Wisconsin to be able to do their ministry more effectively.

Still grappling with where God would have them live, Dave and Jen were working in their Chesterfield home office the morning of September 11, 2001, when the horrific events of 9-11 unfolded. Like the rest of the world, the family was glued to the television and news reports of the terrorist invasion of their home country, the United States, and they realized that the future was forever changed. The tragic consequences of that day led Dave and Jen to do even more praying and seeking God's will, as they struggled where He would have them call "home." As people would ask them where home is, they began answering that it is wherever they happen to be at that moment, all the while realizing that they had no true Home on this earth. Like all believers, their Home is in Heaven where they will live eternally with God when He calls them to Himself.

Over the weeks after 9-11, it became clear to Dave and Jen that they should relocate to Wisconsin. After spending some time between Thanksgiving and Christmas with their families in Indiana, they began making preparations to rent out their Chesterfield home and move to Wisconsin with their boys Chris (who was now a home-schooled high school senior) and soon-to-be 12-year-old Nate.

Christmas was fast-approaching. For a few years now, the Bells had not celebrated Christmas in the traditional American way, turned off by too much emphasis on gifts and parties and not nearly enough focus on the reason for the season. Instead they had spent Christmas Day serving meals to the homeless. Wishing to continue the tradition, they began partnering with a local church to plan an inaugural outreach Christmas event for inner-city Milwaukee, serving meals and distributing clothing and supplies on Christmas Eve and Christmas Day. Excited at the prospect but wondering whether they could possibly drum up enough volunteers to pull it off, the church through Dave and Jen's leadership began advertising the event and seeking volunteers. Keeping their expectations low, they decided that if they could get ten people willing to give up their Christmas Day to serve alongside them that they would be thrilled.

Once more, God taught them a great lesson: when He calls, He provides! Over 60 people committed to helping out in person, and many, many others donated food and clothing items. In fact, Dave and Jen had to turn down volunteer help because there weren't enough jobs for everyone. What a huge blessing, both to those homeless and needy who received love through hot meals and clothing that day and also to those servants who gave of themselves.

And once more, God answered prayers in ways better than Dave and Jen could even have imagined. Hot meals were served to about 250 people off the street that bitterly cold Christmas morning, where Milwaukee temperatures had dipped to ten degrees below zero. Gift boxes of coats, hats, gloves, toys, and food were given to 125 families. And over the course of the four worship services, nearly fifty people made a commitment to Christ.

So many blessings, each story unique and special! But a few stuck out, like the young single mother having walked ten blocks with her three small children in the frigid temperatures to get a Christmas meal that day who was brought to tears when a large box filled with toys and food was given to them. Chris drove the young family home that day and witnessed first-hand their dismal living quarters, a sight he had seen many times overseas but not often in the United States. Then there was a teenage prostitute just trying to survive on the hostile inner city streets with whom the team prayed and planted gospel seeds. The Bells would never forget the four desperately hungry homeless men that came in during the final service who, when it was their turn to get their first meal of the day, instead asked if they could stay and continue singing "Silent Night." Three of those men received their greatest Christmas gift ever that day when they asked Jesus into their hearts.

It was a tradition that would continue and grow for several years, and one the Bells looked forward to each Christmas season. The gifts they received that Christmas and subsequent Wisconsin Christmases were more valuable than anything Santa Claus could have ever brought, blessings of giving God's love and sharing Jesus with some of society's forgotten souls. While it may not have been in the traditional sense, the Bells did indeed celebrate the birth of Christ with family, the family of God's children.

During all those preparations for that first Christmas outreach, Dave and Jen were also in the midst of planning their move to Wisconsin as well as a much-anticipated mission trip to India. Originally they had planned to go to Malawi in January 2002. God clearly closed that door but at the same time opened the doors to minister in India. By this time Dave and Jen had learned their lesson and scrapped their man-made plans for God's plans, and after moving into Sonshine apartments, a unique housing complex for missionaries, on January 11, 2002, they and their sons joined seven others, including Bob Lenz, and winged their way for the first time to India.

CHAPTER 9

India and Malawi

January 2002

People. People. Everywhere people. Throngs of human bodies wound their way through the dusty, trash-filled city streets, clothed in filthy rags and bright colorful saris and every variation in between. Mingling with humankind, yokes of oxen, goats and mangy dogs, donkey carts, and gaunt cattle filled the gaps. Older model cars and taxis jockeyed for position amongst the moving hordes, cut off by the errant motor scooters and rickshaws recklessly winding through the mass of confusion. The honking, incessant honking of horns added to the chaos as drivers tried to force their wills. The undeniable stench of humankind hung in the steamy air, open sewers and decaying animal carcasses adding to the overwhelming malodor.

Beautiful children of God were these Indian people, exotic dark eyes shining in chocolate-hued faces framed by long black hair, yet weighed down by the oppression of poverty and inescapable cultural traditions. While the ancient Hindu caste system was officially outlawed in India during the 1950s, long-held social barriers were not broken down by words written on pieces of paper and Indians still recognized the classes as before. On the bottom rung of the ladder, the lowliest of the low, the poorest of the poor: the Dalits or "Untouchables."

Add to that the burden of the dowry system, where the family of a young girl must come up with an outlandish bride price in order for their daughter to marry. Because so many families cannot afford the dowry, every few minutes in India baby girls are abandoned by desperately poor parents to save the disgrace of not being able to pay the future dowry.

And on every corner a colorful shrine or altar to one of the countless Hindu gods, draped in wilting flowers, the brilliant hues and exquisite artwork seemingly hiding the true spiritual darkness of a people desperately in need of Jesus.

Even with all their third world travel experience and trip research, the Bells were not quite prepared for this sensory overload that assaulted them. Welcome to India, a place unlike any other on the globe.

In the weeks leading up to their January 2002 trip, news of clashes between India and neighboring Pakistan had filled the airwaves. Family and friends warned them against going, fearful that as Christian missionaries they may be caught in the crossfire. Of course, with India being a "closed" country, with an anti-conversion law that made it illegal for citizens to convert to Christianity, they weren't going in the official capacity as "missionaries." They were tourists, on a mission to share the gospel with as many Indians as they could reach in the short two weeks they would be visiting.

God had clearly called them to go, and unless He stopped it the group of eleven was determined to obey that call. And so on January 11, the team boarded a plane from the deep-freeze of Wisconsin and 24+ hours later found themselves on the tarmac in suffocatingly hot and humid Hyderabad, an Islamic city in central India where Christians comprise a meager 2% of the population.

The initial plan for the week in Hyderabad was to share in the secular schools. Even though the city is almost completely Muslim, the schools there were started by Christians and therefore sharing about

Christ would be permitted. The team was thrilled about this opportunity to reach so many Islamic schoolchildren in the school setting, students who had never heard the message of a living and loving God or of the forgiveness and salvation that awaits those who receive Him.

But, as so often happens, those plans had to be scrapped when they discovered the public schools were all on vacation to celebrate Pongal, the Hindu festival of the harvest. Instead of sharing with countless Muslim students, they were scheduled to speak at six Christian schools instead. Thinking that their message wouldn't have nearly the impact there, the team soon learned that the overwhelming majority of children in the Christian schools were not Christian at all, but were sent to those schools by their Hindu and Muslim families due to the quality of education there. By the end of the week, Bob had spoken and the Bells and other team members had shared in song and testimony to over 8000 students!

Again, God's plan had trumped theirs. Those whom God wanted to hear the gospel had. And while the team had no way of knowing for sure how many lives were eternally impacted, they felt sure that countless seeds of knowledge and faith had been planted and the message of the Good News presented in this land of oppression and physical and spiritual poverty.

A middle-aged Indian man named Lousan was the team's cook while in Hyderabad. Lousan's mother, who lived with his family, had been bitten by a rabid dog and was intensely suffering from rabies, and toward the end of the week Lousan asked the team to come pray for her. What a shock for many on the team as they made their way behind a nice hotel walking down a narrow alley leading one of the most destitute neighborhoods they had ever experienced! Lousan's home, shared by his wife, daughter, and grandson as well as his mother, was a ten-foot-square shack with a dirt floor and very thin thatched roof. One person's arms could have easily carried all of this family's possessions. The team prayed over the dying mother, barely more than a tiny skeleton curled up on the dirt floor. It was a heart-wrenching image that would be forever etched into the minds of those Americans.

The second week in India was to be spent in the east coast village of Bapatla, a seven-hour train trip. Riding the train across India's terrain was a cultural experience in itself, but the train stations where the team stopped were eye-popping. Having already seen much poverty and the deplorable living conditions endured by most Indian people, they were still ill-prepared for the hundreds of homeless people sleeping inside the filthy, crowded train stations, countless cripples and beggars constantly circling the missionaries, hounding them for money.

Arriving in Bapatla about midnight and assuming everyone at the orphanage where they would be ministering would be asleep, what a beautiful surprise it was to be greeted by some of the 120 children. They lined the entrance holding candles and presented the team with strings of flowers, all the while singing, "Auntie, Uncle, welcome to you." After the long, difficult day of traveling, such a special, heart-warming welcome brought tears to the Americans' eyes.

The four days the missionaries stayed at the REACH (Rural Education and Children's Health) Home in India were filled with loving on the precious children who lived there. Many varied circumstances brought them to the home: both parents dead, their mother gone and the father did not want them, or their family simply could not afford to feed them and so they were abandoned. So many heart-breaking and humbling stories!

Before leaving the US, God had provided over $60,000 worth of medical supplies for the team to take to India. Knowing there would definitely be a need for those supplies but not sure just where to donate them, in Bapatla God's plan became clear. A brand new hospital, made possible by a very generous donor who gave $150,000 for its building, was just one week away from completion. What a blessing this medical facility would be to the local villagers, making care much more accessible by eliminating the previously necessary 75-mile trip to the nearest hospital. But the hospital staff had not been able to yet obtain many supplies needed before opening, basic supplies such sutures and bandages which "just so happened" to be among the supplies the team had brought with them. God continued to amaze!

While touring the new hospital facilities, the REACH director Kusuma shared about a young unwed mother who had requested to leave her three-day-old infant at the orphanage because she was unable to care for it. Very reluctantly, Kusuma had denied the request because the Hindu government prohibited placement of infants in Christian institutions. The next morning in the cloak of early morning darkness, the girl had brought the baby anyway and left.

Holding the newborn in his arms, Bob immediately named her Grace. A few days later, Grace's grandparents came to the orphanage for the little girl, hoping to keep her. The local culture would make that very difficult, as unwed mothers are shunned and a baby born outside of wedlock is treated as an outcast and considered a disgrace to her family. Yet another heart-breaking story that would forever change the mission team.

What an eye-opener India had been! And so very heart-breaking for the Bells, each one of them struggling with the unfairness and desperation in their own way. Nate wanting to bring home every precious little baby he fell in love with at the orphanages, Dave and Jen falling on their knees before their Creator, asking Him if perhaps THIS was the ministry to which He was calling them, and their frustrating heartache when God answered them clearly, that no, not this one, somehow impressing upon their hearts that rescuing children was their calling but not in this place. With such poverty and spiritual darkness amidst some of the most beautiful people the Bells had ever met, they knew that they would be back, hopefully sooner rather than later, with more teams through the new Life Promotions Missions program.

After arriving back in Wisconsin, Dave and Jen became fully integrated into the Life Promotions staff. Besides heading up the missions program, Dave became the building manager and Jen the office manager. Their plates were full and often over-flowing, planning mission trips and keeping the daily Life Promotions operations running smoothly.

March 2002 found them traveling once more, this time back to Mexico. The connections the Bells had made during their time serving with Companeros led them to visit Rancho Sordo Mudo, Spanish for "deaf mute ranch" in Baja California, Mexico, just south of Tijuana. Founded by Ed and Margaret Everett in the late 1960s, RSM is a free boarding school for deaf children. While the children are taught how to read and write and to communicate in sign language so they will be able to learn a trade and become contributing members of society, the more important goal is to teach the children about God's love for them and give them hope for the future.

Dave, Jen, Chris, and Nate immediately fell in love with the children and ministry at the ranch, and they knew this would also be a perfect mission opportunity for future Life Promotions teams. Love and compassion for these happy, smiling children quickly broke down whatever communication barriers there were. While the children wormed their way into the hearts of them all, Chris and Nate especially loved playing and working with these special kids. It didn't take long for the Bell boys to learn sign language and become buddies with all of them.

Whatever was needed at Rancho Sordo Mudo, the Bells did; building, remodeling, cleaning, cooking, as well as spending time teaching and working with the children filled the days at the school. It was an amazing experience that the Bells would share with other mission teams in coming years, and while they worked hard they also left for Wisconsin refreshed and energized from their time at RSM.

The spring of 2002 brought a huge change to the Bell family. Chris turned 18 and was graduating from high school. Dave and Jen could already sense the transition ahead as they celebrated Chris's graduation with friends and family at an ice cream party at the Sonshine House. Having chosen to begin college classes at Johnson

University in Knoxville, Tennessee that fall, Chris was excited to start his adult life, and Dave and Jen, while excited for him, felt all too well the winds of change blowing.

But there wasn't a lot of time to think about that. Planning for Lifest in July was at full throttle, and soon following that at the end of July was a new outreach in the works. Dubbed "Hopefest," this one-day street festival in the inner city of Milwaukee was a new venture for Life Promotions and the Bells. Vendors had to be secured, stages set up, games organized, and speakers booked, not to mention food and volunteers. It was a big undertaking with a lot of question marks, but one thing was for certain: the message of Christ's love and acceptance would be presented clearly, and many, both those receiving the Word as well as those sharing it, would be blessed. So Dave and Jen put the logistics into place and gave the event to God.

Exhausted yet revitalized after Lifest and Hopefest the month before followed by a whirlwind of activity and trip to Tennessee to settle Chris in at Johnson, Dave and Jen took their second trip to Africa on August 24, 2002, this time to the country of Malawi. They left with mixed emotions -- excited anticipation and broken hearts. Pat's cancer was winning the battle for her earthly body, and Jen had just helped make arrangements for her mother to come home from the hospital and into hospice care. Times like these were a painful reality of being a missionary, times when they felt the difficult tug-of-war between family commitments and God's calling. While they knew in their hearts that God had their full allegiance and obedience to Him always trumped their human desires, it still was very difficult for them to go ahead with their trip, and it didn't help matters when many friends and family openly questioned their decision to continue on to Malawi as planned. But Jen's mother, even in the last stages of her days on earth, insisted that they go and do what God had called them to do.

Kissing her dying mother good-bye in her childhood home that late summer day, it would be the final time Jen would see Pat on this side of eternity.

And so with heavy hearts, Dave, Jen, and Nate obeyed the Lord's calling and boarded an airplane destined for Malawi, a nation ravaged by AIDS, where one out of every three adults were dying of this tragic disease, leaving hundreds of children orphaned every day and ultimately facing the same fate as their parents. A nation suffering from a famine of epic proportions, both physically and spiritually. A nation of some of the friendliest, warmest, and most welcoming people the Bells had ever encountered.

As with the trip to Rancho Sordu Mudo, this venture was in part an exploratory trip for the Bells as they anticipated perhaps taking a youth mission team there in the future. With that goal in mind, they had asked their host William Mposa to give them a well-rounded experience of what Malawi was like and he wonderfully accommodated their request.

Several hundred students at five different schools, some private schools "blessed" by Malawi standards and others crowded public schools with limited funds and outdated equipment, heard Dave and Jen share the gospel clearly and openly with them. They told about Jesus in remote rural villages, sharing Jesus wherever they went and even on Malawi television, which they jokingly dubbed "MTV." And then there were the prisons...

Oh, the prisons! Conditions in those women's prisons they visited in Chichiri and Zomba were beyond deplorable. It amazed Dave and Jen that the 65 women and juveniles housed there could even survive the filth and depravity. And yet, sharing a message of hope and a simple bar of soap with these forgotten elements of Malawi society brought blessings to the Bells as they witnessed the openness of these prisoners to the love of the only One they had to cling to and access to the only freedom worth having.

One woman particularly tugged at their hearts, a teenage girl who had been in prison for six months helplessly awaiting a hearing that would be held perhaps weeks or months or even years later. What made her story unique and especially wrenching was that she was imprisoned with her two young children, a four-year-old toddler and an eighteen-month-old that she was still nursing. Here she was, sharing a small area with over a dozen other women, all filthy and receiving one very meager meal per day, trying to care for these precious children. Seeing adults suffer in such circumstances is painful, but seeing innocent children living in those conditions was almost unbearable for Dave and Jen.

Another visit was to the Soldier's Home where over 100 elderly men and women were raising their grandchildren due to the rapidly-disappearing generation of their adult children succumbing to AIDS. Nate brought youthful energy playing with the children there, and the tired adults delighted in watching the smiles and laughter the Bells brought during their brief stay, sharing some moments of joy and a lifetime of hope in Jesus in the midst of their miserable circumstances here on earth.

Much to their amazement, during their stay in Malawi they were invited to visit a Muslim training center. Not knowing what to expect and having limited experience with the Islam religion, Dave and Jen were a bit nervous about this visit. They needn't have been, as it turned out the center was a place where women came to learn to sew in order to earn a living for themselves and their families. Fifty Muslim women came to hear the Americans share about themselves and about a God who loved them and died for them. The Bells had been specifically instructed not to mention "Jesus" in the sharing, so carefully they picked their words as they gave their testimonies.

As they finished speaking, four women began singing a song in Chechewa, the lyrics about Christ going to the cross for our sins. Soon the entire room joined them in singing a song of praise. Dave and Jen discovered that these women were believers, Muslim in culture but Christian in faith and very open to the message of a living God. Seeds were planted that day!

The highlight of the Malawi trip, especially for Jen, was visiting the Open Arms Orphanage in Blantyre, a special home for forty children up to the age of two years. Playing with and loving on these little ones, many of them orphaned due to the rampant AIDS epidemic, the Bells' hearts broke as the staff shared the shocking statistics: over half of the babies that came to the orphanage died before they had been there a month.

While it was a joy to be able to take some supplies, balls, and toys for the toddlers, the Bells ached to be able to do more. And it pained them to realize that Open Arms was just one of hundreds of such homes in Malawi. These little ones were just the tip of an iceberg of pain and suffering in this part of the world.

It had been a great trip, but by the time Dave, Jen, and Nate boarded the plane they were definitely ready to get home to family and friends. The always-long and arduous trip home was even more so this time, with several hours sitting around in foreign airports. One can only play so many rounds of Rummy. Arriving back in Wisconsin late on a Tuesday night, they received word on Thursday that Pat had taken a turn for the worse. Still fighting jetlag, they decided to head back to Indiana early Friday morning and at 4:30 a.m., just as they were about to leave, Jen received the phone call that her mother had defeated her battle with cancer and was finally pain- and tear-free, now resting comfortably in her Savior's arms.

While it was certainly not a surprise, Pat's death was still a huge blow to the family, and the next several days were a whirlwind of grief and planning, celebrating Pat's gain but mourning the unfillable hole she left behind. Pat's death was yet another stark reminder of the urgency to share the gospel with as many as possible so that all may have the opportunity to believe and share Heaven's glorious eternity.

CHAPTER 10

Bringing the Light

January 2003

Memories. So many memories, a few painful but mostly fond…memories.

Winding their way through the gravestones in the Sugar Grove Community Church's country cemetery, Dave held his mourning wife's hand as they walked back to the car. Just being here in this place brought the memories flooding back. Although they had traveled many tens of thousands of miles since their Indiana childhood days, there really was no place like home.

Smiling through her tears of grief, Jen looked up into the bright blue crisp fall sky dotted by marshmallow clouds. A huge transition awaited all of them, but especially Earl. Losing the love of his life and the mother of his children would undeniably be the hardest thing he had ever faced. Yet despite their grief, this day was a celebration of a beautiful life of one of God's own who, after agonizing months of suffering, was now Home. Jen knew her mother was in Heaven, where she would join her someday. And that promise, despite the pain in her heart, made her smile.

And it also renewed the sense of urgency for Dave and Jen. In the scheme of Eternity, life here on earth is very short and so many, so very many people were still lost in the darkness without Jesus. They needed the Light! So many to tell, so little time.

Although Pat had crossed over to spend eternity with her Lord, her legacy on earth would live on throughout Jen's life. One of the most treasured and memorable lessons were these words of wisdom, learned through Pat's own personal struggles, that Pat had shared with her daughter after receiving Christ as her Savior so many years ago: "When life is so overwhelming, just one word is all you need to speak and hold onto. 'JESUS.'" Only God knew what an anchor that teaching would be during many unseen future storms that lay ahead, and how many times Jen would cling to her mother's advice and hold onto Jesus!

Following Pat's funeral and all that surrounded it, the Bells hit the ground running when they arrived back home in Wisconsin, with mission trips to plan, Life Promotion events to coordinate, and finances to raise. The calendar that had been on "pause" for a few days was now back on "play," and the days were filled with innumerable tasks to do with seemingly not enough hours to do them. But as always, God somehow multiplied their time and life steamed ahead.

Christmas Day 2002 once more found the Bells partnering with Blessed Hope Church serving the homeless and poor in inner-city Milwaukee. Over 300 people came in off the cold streets to enjoy a warm Christmas meal, receive canned goods and presents, and most importantly carry home in their hearts the greatest gift the world has ever know -- Jesus! After weeks of wondering whether they would have enough volunteers and food donations, God incredibly provided both and gave the entire team a huge boost as the Kingdom gained 75 new or recommitted believers that day. A success both in earthly terms and, more importantly, eternal ones.

Just one month later Dave, Jen, and Nate, leading a thirteen-person team of doctors, nurses, students, handymen, and many willing hearts, found themselves landing in Bombay, India, to catch a connecting flight to Hyderabad with plans to minister in the same area they had visited the year before. Amongst their luggage they carried thirteen bags filled with $200,000 worth of medical supplies that had been donated for the trip. While Dave knew full well that their cargo might cause some delays along the way, they trusted that if God had graciously provided the donation, He would also pave the way for its safe arrival into India.

Twelve of the team members breezed through customs without incident, and all except Dave, who as team leader stayed behind until all were cleared, had made it outside the airport and were awaiting the bus to take them to their connecting flight to Hyderabad which was departing in less than an hour. But that last doctor carrying the final bag was stopped by a wary security guard. The contents of that thirteenth bag included several donated blood pressure cuffs, which just so happened to look like time bomb dials on the x-ray machine.

As Dave watched the drama unfold at the check-point, he was soon summoned back to the customs area and informed that the Head of Security would like to see him in his office. Uh-oh.

The team doctor, allowed to leave when Dave went back, quickly exited the airport and shared the situation with his colleagues waiting outside. The team circled up in prayer just outside the airport, petitioning God for Dave's safety and clearance into the country.

No one on that team was praying harder than Dave himself, stories of foreign persecution and prisons filling his mind as he was led through the busy airport. He knew all too well about the Indian Hindu government's increased persecution of Christians in recent months. Initial panic was quickly replaced by a deep sense of peace that God was still in control and this was His battle, and Dave prayed that God would calm his heart, give him wisdom, and put on his tongue the proper words to defuse what could be an explosive situation.

Closing his office door behind him, the officer demanded to see permits and forms that Dave supposedly "needed" but did not have. It quickly became apparent to Dave what the man was after: an admission that this was a Christian outreach, which would give him grounds to confiscate the luggage, and a bribe. Dave was not going to give him either.

The discussion became very heated at times, with some verbal outbursts in the native language of Telegu that Dave was glad he could not understand. Dave was not budging; he felt very clearly that God would not have him offer up a bribe for the passage of His goods. The officer talked of bringing the entire team and their luggage back in for further questioning and examination. Just then, the guard who had initially stopped the doctor began arguing with his supervisor that the group should be allowed to pass unhindered. Once more a heated argument ensued, this time between the guard and his supervising officer, that Dave could understand only by the tone of voice. Suddenly the officer pointed to the door and angrily yelled, "Get out!" He didn't have to tell Dave twice, and the security guard quickly led him out of the airport.

What a relief! Hearts still pounding from the harrowing experience, the team boarded the bus but had already missed their scheduled flight. Despite the delay, Dave believed the two-hour wait for the next plane to Hyderabad was worth it, as the team saw God's power at work so early in the trip. And it also taught the team of schedule- and goal-minded Americans that not only is God's schedule not necessarily the same as theirs, but that in most other countries time is not viewed in the same way, that a designated time is more of a suggestion than an actual commitment.

The team would learn many lessons on that trip, with Dave and Jen as first-time mission team leaders learning many as well. The American mindset is so task-oriented that mission team members often feel frustrated when they aren't doing what they define as "mission" work. What they must realize, Dave and Jen told them, is that Indian eyes are always on them, watching their every move. They are ministering in every interaction with every person they meet, a real-life reminder that no matter what any of us is doing, we are always interpreted to be setting an example of Christ, whether good or bad, to those around us.

In Hyderabad, the team shared at a local seminary and then provided a free medical clinic for the students and their families, seeing 125 patients before finally closing the doors at midnight. The next day the team took 400 pounds of rice and wheat, their medical supplies, and God's love to the Hope Slum village on the outskirt of Hyderabad.

Hope Slum was a village of 175 homes packed into an area about a quarter of the size of a football field, tiny homes perhaps 10'x10' with walls of mud and roofs of tarps or cardboard. In India's caste society, this had been home for twenty years to a group of the lowest class, the Untouchables. In all their extensive travels, Dave and Jen had never seen the poverty they witnessed at Hope Slum village.

Walking between the homes, Jen noticed a little girl about eight years old, eyes dark with the desperation of being unloved, standing off alone and shunned by the others, an outcast even in this village of outcasts. As Jen drew near, she saw the signs of leprosy, and knelt down and wrapped her arms around the emaciated child. Initially the little girl tried to rip herself away, the terrified look in her eyes revealing her fear of what might happen if someone touched her. Jen didn't flinch, holding her close and crying with her. Instantly, that child melted into Jen's arms and would hardly let go, leaving the Bells to suspect it was the first human touch she had experienced in a very long time.

It was a reality check for the rest of the team as they watched, and they suddenly understood just why they had come. Passing out medicines and food were nothing compared to the hope and love they were passing out. For that moment, these rich Americans became part of the lives of these children of God, feeling an inkling of their pain and yet seeing the pride and dignity in these people despite their extreme poverty. Lives were impacted through experiences like these, not only those in the Hope Slum but even more so the lives of those "spoiled" American missionaries.

Once more, the train stations along the seven-hour trip to Bapatla provided more eye-opening experiences. The team of missionaries would be operating from the same home that the Bells had visited the previous January, REACH Home, where the team members would leave a large part of their hearts by the time they departed, as they fell in love with the 200 children and the compassionate couple who operated the orphanage.

Free medical camps were one of the main outreaches for the trip, and the team assisted a local hospital in conducting several in area villages, schools, and orphanages. Over 1000 patients were able to be examined by a doctor, many of them for the first time in their lives, with maladies ranging from heartburn to incurable diseases such as cancer and multiple sclerosis. While it was gratifying for these American health professionals to be able to help so many people, it was heartbreaking for them to grapple with the sobering fact that they could not fix each problem, and they knew that many they examined at the medical camp would have their lives cut short. Exhausted and humbled, but grateful for the blessing to serve, the team left India having accomplished much, yet a mere drop in the ocean of spiritual darkness and physical need.

Each trip abroad found the Bells more certain of their calling into this ministry and rejoicing at the opportunities God continued to place before them. Although they often wondered from where the funds to sustain the ministry would come, God proved over and over again that He was their Provider and Sustainer of all needs. For two people who in their previous lives (which, although less than four years had passed, seemed light-years ago) had been control-freaks, trusting God had become second-nature. While letting go and letting God was not always easy, He had never let them down. Slowly and surely financial support continued to come in, and Dave and Jen never took any of that generosity for granted.

They hadn't been back home in Wisconsin long before they received a call from their realtor that their Chesterfield, Indiana home had sold. Once more, God had provided the perfect buyer at the perfect time, and in March 2003 they signed the paperwork and once more felt freed from another earthly tie.

In March 2003, Dave and Jen led their first Life Promotions youth missions trip to Rancho Sordo Mudo, the deaf school in Mexico. For many of these young students, this was their first trip outside their comfortable American lifestyle. On their initial trip to this boarding school of 30 in Guadalupe, Mexico, Dave and Jen had known at once that this would be a great outreach for young mission teams, and their week there did not disappoint. The team members immediately clicked with the young Mexican children, many of them able to use their school-learned Spanish skills for the first time as well as learning sign language while there. Teaching, working, playing, and especially loving on the happy students at the ranch made for a wonderful week for everyone.

Back in the States, the next couple of months would be spent gearing up for Lifest in July. In April 2003, Dave, while still on staff as building manager for Life Promotions, was also named the Associate Director of Lifest, greatly increasing his responsibilities for the huge event. At that year's festival, where the gospel would be shared through music and testimony to as many as 18,000 people per day, Dave was coordinating efforts with Habitat for Humanity to raise awareness for the plight of the poor and homeless. A home, being built for a single mother and her son, would be partially constructed on the Lifest grounds and then after the festival moved to its permanent location nearby. Many youth in attendance would have a chance to serve and be the hands of Christ to this young mother as they drove nails into her new home. The entire Lifest event was a monumental undertaking, and Dave and Jen, who was still serving as Life Promotions office manager and as such in charge of ticket sales and coordinating many of the logistics required for the event, spent long days preparing for and pulling off what turned out to be another wildly successful Christian outreach.

Next up was Hopefest, the one-day street festival in inner city Milwaukee at the end of July. Being the second year, the Bells and their team worked out many of the kinks from the previous year's Hopefest and it was another wonderful day of fun activities and sharing of the gospel to many who had never heard the Good News. Following Hopefest, for the first time in the past couple of years, the Bells had a few months to recharge in the States before gearing up for more international mission work.

While Nate, now ready to begin eighth grade, had been traveling with his parents and homeschooling along the way, Chris had stayed behind pursuing his degree at Johnson University in Tennessee. It was there at Johnson, in October 2002, that he began dating Ariel. Ariel had been a high school cheerleader at Daleville High School in Indiana and Chris had met her through his best friend Andy while still in high school. After his freshman year at Johnson, Chris decided to move back to Indiana and finish his schooling at Anderson University. Ariel moved back as well, and in the summer of 2003 the two of them packed her small car full of their belongings and returned north to their old stomping grounds. Chris enrolled for the fall semester at AU and soon found employment at the county youth center working with troubled teens. Dave and Jen could see that Chris and Ariel were very much in love and would have a future together, that he was an adult now and striking out on his own. They couldn't help but feel a twinge of sadness mixed with pride as they watched their eldest son stretch his wings and take flight, a wonderful young man of God.

The day after their third Christmas Day outreach of serving ham and hope to over 400 impoverished folks living on the streets of Milwaukee, on December 26, 2003 Dave, Jen, and Nate left for their first trip to the Dominican Republic with a team of junior-high students. Normally Dave and Jen would scope out possible mission destinations, but when God opened doors through Dave's niece Karen Miller, who was serving in the DR at that time as a missionary teaching English to the locals, for the trip, they jumped at the opportunity. Feeling confident and, as some might think, perhaps a little crazy, they threw their customary caution to the wind and took their first team of 13-14-year-olds to the Dominican Republic.

What a great blessing this trip turned out to be! The young teenagers brought energy and enthusiasm and a willingness to be vessels for Jesus. Since it was over the holiday, Karen was able to spend the week with them also blessing them with her translation skills. Visiting many extremely poor villages surrounding Azua, the team was able to bless families with food, medical supplies, and sports equipment, all of which had been donated. And giving out these items allowed them an audience with which to share the gospel. The promise of a Savior who loves them and the hope that message brings was well-received by over 1200 people who simply struggled to survive from day to day.

In one of the villages, they met a woman in her fifties, her body ravished by polio and cerebral palsy, lying on a filthy mattress surrounded by her few meager possessions, where she had lain most of her life since being struck by those debilitating diseases 40 years before. She had rarely been in the sunshine nor felt the coolness of a fresh breeze, and now since the death of her mother and the recent demise of one sister, she received very little attention except the most basic care from her remaining sister. Yet despite her suffering, what joy shone from her eyes as she knew Jesus and shared how much she loved Him and He her and how she knew He is always with her.

The team was so struck by her witness that the women and girls in the group returned to her house the next day to give her a bath and do some basic cleaning around her bed, where they were sickened to find a mouse nest and cockroaches in her bedding. But they also found a very peaceful soul, a believer that through her misery shone a bright light of faith that those young Americans would forever remember, and leaving her that day they all knew that Jesus was holding her much tighter than any of them ever could.

Drugs and alcohol have a powerful stronghold on many in the Dominican Republic, as they do all over the world. Visiting a rehab center, Dave brought the light of Jesus to several young men who were fighting Satan's hold on them. By using glow sticks they had brought along, which these young men had never before seen, to the awe and amazement of these tortured young men Dave illustrated how God needs to break us of ourselves and the things of this world and invite

Him into our hearts before His light can shine. It was a powerful demonstration and those young men that day made a commitment to the Lord. Asking if they had Bibles, the team felt helpless and guilty discovering that none of these tortured young men owned a copy of the Word of God while they thought of the numerous Bibles they each had easy access to back in the States. The next day, the team returned to the rehab center and left knowing each of these new believers had his very own Bible to read.

Undoubtedly, this trip was a life-changer for the group of young teens, one they would remember long after they returned home in early January 2004. Dave and Jen had a couple of weeks to regroup and catch up on Life Promotions responsibilities as well as squeeze in a visit with their families.

Soon the Bells were off once again, leaving January 27, 2004, for their third trip to India. Once more they would take a Life Promotions team to Andreh Pradesh to minister to the children at the REACH Home in Bapatla, as well as the surrounding villages. Traveling with them for the first part of the trip was Bob Lenz and Number One Fan, a local band, to do concerts and rallies in the nearby city of Hyderabad. Each day Bob and the band shared music and testimonies with about 3000 college students, culminating in a city-wide rally the final day. Despite the danger that the Muslim/Hindu government's "anti-conversion" law might mar the plans and hinder the team, God intervened and provided many wonderful opportunities, and thousands of Indians heard for the first time the life-saving message of Jesus.

March 20, 2004 found the Bells heading back to Rancho Sordo Mudo in Mexico with a mission team, to work with the deaf children living there. As that team headed home after a wonderful week at RSM, Dave and Jen picked up a new team from the airport and drove them to the home, back-to-back teams over colleges' Spring Breaks, opportunities for service and ministry and for young believers to see God working first-hand through Life Promotions missions.

Hectic schedules had become the norm for Dave and Jen, yet they were thriving in the midst of the sometimes chaotic days, constantly licking and turning, trying to keep up and forge ahead. Darkness was rampant and time was short.

For bringing the light.

CHAPTER 11

Little Did They Know

July 2004

G od certainly had a sense of humor. Of that, Dave was sure.

Opening wide a door of opportunity for the Bells to minister in Kenya, God surely must have been snickering. KENYA. Yet another of those African countries that Dave had been loathe to visit.

Although, Dave would have to admit, their time in Ghana and Malawi had changed his perspective a little. After all, Africa had millions of people who were living in spiritual darkness, many of whom had never heard the gospel, a continent where the fields were rich for harvest yet the workers were pitifully few. But still, not Africa again....

Through the connections of a Wisconsin friend, the three Bells and eight others left Wisconsin in July 2004 for their first foray into Kenya. Little did they know the future that this eastern African nation in the center of the globe halfway across the world would eventually hold for them.

Having been told they would be staying at the HEART compound, Dave and Jen naively wondered why they would be housed at a medical facility. Bumping their way through the compound gate, Dave and Jen smiled at each other as the realization hit them both at the same time—HEART was not a hospital, but instead an acronym for Health Education Africa Resource Team.

The team was especially grateful for their HEART host when they discovered that the Kenyan host pastor had arranged for them to head out for their Kitale area destination in western Kenya late the next afternoon in an eight-seat van for the team of eleven. Thankfully the HEART host interceded and offered their driver and larger vehicle to the team and convinced them to leave earlier than planned.

Grueling! There was no other way to describe that drive. What they were told would be an eight-hour drive turned out to be twelve hours of teeth-jarring bouncing and white-knuckled driving over the roughest roads the team had ever experienced. Feeling it nothing less than a miracle when they finally arrived in the village just outside of Kitale, the team was mentally and physically exhausted and ready to fall into bed. But as the vehicle pulled into the village at midnight, the whole village was waiting in the dark to greet them, waiting where they had all day for a mzungu, Swahili for "white man," sermon.

Dave, Jen, & Nate   2004

What else was there to do but preach?! Only through God-given strength were these mzungus able to share the gospel with these villagers hungry for truth. A few of the men obliged and preached until about 2:00 a.m., thinking they had satisfied the Kenyans and hoping to get some rest when they were informed that dinner awaited them. What else was there to do but eat and fellowship with the excited villagers? It was a very long night indeed!

The next few days brought the team of Americans memorable first-hand experiences of rural life in Kenya. Treating the missionaries like royalty, the villagers had set up a kitchen-of-sorts in a chicken coop just for the occasion so they could make their specialty chapatti bread for the team. Dubbed the "chapatti shack," the team watched in dismay as the cooks cheerfully flipped chapattis while simultaneously shooing the chickens away. By the time the team left, most had suffered ill effects, with less than desirable toilet facilities to cope with those effects, from eating chapattis and other local foods similarly prepared.

Leaving that village, they headed to the other side of Kenya to a small village of Masii. Here the team connected with Dr. Stanley Mutunga, PhD, who had started a program assisting AIDS orphans, and were stunned to see firsthand the devastating impact AIDS was having on the country of Kenya. Their parents dying off in staggering numbers, hundreds of children were daily being left behind with no one to care for them. These orphaned children pulled at the heartstrings of the entire team, but Dave and Jen were especially unsettled by their plight. In a culture which placed so much emphasis on family connections and tribal influence, what kind of future would these innocent children face? They couldn't shake the feeling of helplessness that overcame them at the fate of these littlest ones.

Walking back to the hotel that afternoon, deep in thought as well as emotionally and physically drained by the past few days of teaching and hazardous traveling, Dave's back started to hurt. Over a short amount of time the twinge turned into intense, excruciating pain. Realizing that the nearest hospital was a 45-minute drive away, Stanley insisted that they take Dave to the hospital. Breaking out in a sweat and heaving with agony, Dave was so desperate to get medical help that he tried to get out of the vehicle at a police checkpoint and force his way through. Jen held him down and tried to calm her nearly-delirious husband as the doctor was finally able to reason with the police and the vehicle was allowed to pass through.

By the time they arrived at the government hospital in Machakos, Dave was nearly blind with pain and screaming out so loudly that it was scaring everyone. Being told there was no doctor there at that moment nearly sent him over the edge. Stanley telephoned a contact at a hotel just outside of town and was told that there was a doctor who was on call for hotel guests. Stumbling back into the vehicle, they were driven to the nearby hotel where the doctor came in the room, briefly looked at Dave, and declared that he was having a kidney stone attack. And, this being Kenya, he had no medication with him, so Dave dragged himself back into the car and they followed this doctor to his office in town.

The doctor's "office" consisted of a closet-sized room with a chair and small bed dimly lit by a dangling light bulb. Dave was given some diuretics to help pass the stone and was also administered some very strong pain meds, Jen watching every move the doctor made, making sure that the drugs given were not out of date and the syringe and needle came from unopened packaging. As Dave lay in anguish waiting for the drugs to take effect, the physician struck up a conversation with Jen asking her what they were doing in Kenya. As Jen shared the plight of the orphans in Masii, the doctor was deeply touched and volunteered to go work with them and provide medical care, a service that would last for many years to come.

Finally feeling some relief, Dave and Jen were driven back to the hotel where Dave stumbled into the lobby and pronounced he was doing great. Nate laughed as his drugged-up Dad provided some free entertainment that evening, the powerful pain medications having made him quite loopy. Dave would never remember most of that evening. But what he DID remember was getting out of bed in the middle of the night and passing that kidney stone, and it's a good bet that everyone in the nearby rooms knew it too! Dave would suffer several kidney stone attacks over his lifetime and pass many stones, but none would be as memorable as this first one.

Returning to the States, Dave and Jen both knew this trip to Kenya had been a life-changer. They weren't sure yet just how, but they could feel it in the depths of their souls, and the faces of those precious orphans traveled home with them. God had struck a chord for Kenya deep within the Bells that resonated long after they returned to Wisconsin.

Little did they know that in a couple of years HEART would become much more to them than a place to lay their head at night and Kenya much more than a mission trip destination. Looking back years later, Dave and Jen would clearly see how the hand of God had been all over this initial trip, laying a foundation for the future and preparing their hearts for the ministry He had called them to do. They weren't ready just yet.

But little did they know...

CHAPTER 12

The Equipping

Fall 2004 – Spring 2006

Seasons of a person's life take on their own personalities as people settle into God's plan for them at that moment. For the Bells, life eventually fell into a new rhythm…working with Life Promotions in Wisconsin punctuated by frequent trips leading international teams on short-term missions. God knew and the Bells would soon learn that the eighteen months following their return from Kenya was to be a season of equipping.

When God calls, He equips. Dave and Jen had witnessed that many times already in the years since He had called them into missionary work. That equipping can and does take many different forms for different people and circumstances, but in the Bells' case God's equipping very often came through experiences and people God led to cross their paths.

Januarys would find them leading a team back to India. No matter how many times they went, India always took their breath away, in more ways than one. Immediately after stepping off the plane onto the Bombay tarmac, there was simply no way to prepare for the sensory assault that they experienced. Weaving through the crowded terminal into the equally crowded city streets, pouring into the steamy thoroughfares to intermingle with the filthy yet beautiful hordes of

Indian people, each arrival in India was fraught with familiarity and yet a unique strangeness to which Dave, Jen, and Nate never became accustomed. The pungent odor hanging in the hot, dank air was a mysterious mixture of curry and urine, seasoned by incense and the smells of sewage, cooking meat, and decaying bodies.

And the sounds, oh the sounds of India! Honking vehicle horns were a constant, the huge, loud bus horns, car horns, bicycle horns, and rickshaw horns combined with the mooing of cattle, squawking of ravens, and the shrill metallic chants wafting from the countless Hindu temples created an indescribable constant, crazy cacophony. For a blessed few hours between midnight and four in the morning, a welcome yet eerie quietness descended on the city only to be broken in the predawn hours by the cat-like whining music and crowing roosters, an uncommon alarm clock that would wake even the soundest sleeper. By the time the sun arose, the city was wide awake and the whole chaos began again.

But it was the people that brought Dave and Jen back year after year, these precious strikingly handsome children of God cloaked in an invisible oppression of darkness in a country of seemingly constant sunshine. An oppression of desperate poverty, indefinable depravity, indescribable physical suffering, and cultural chains all creating a palpable darkness that silently cried out for relief. A relief that Dave and Jen and the very few Christians (1%) in that area knew could only come from Jesus. It was what brought them back to India again and again.

Struggling with the unfairness of life in India and frustrated with the plight of those born through no fault of their own into the Dalit caste and considered too low to be of any value, the Bells wrangled to understand how a good loving God could allow this to happen. It was an unanswerable question, they knew, but still they grappled with the reality that many Indians lived each day. And yet, they fell in love — with the Indian people, the food, and many aspects of the culture. God allowed them to be submersed in the love of those minority Christians who were willing to sacrifice so much to be His servants, and they marveled at the witness of these bold souls who were daily being persecuted for their belief. Oftentimes Dave and Jen would wonder whether perhaps this is where God was leading them for long-term missionary work, to serve alongside these saints bringing light to the tortured souls of the Indian people.

But more than anything, Dave, Jen, and Nate fell in love with the children, those adorable smiling orphans at REACH Home who melted their hearts as they reached for their hands. Leaving them behind to return home, they discovered first-hand the inevitable pain of returning the following January to find many of these children that they'd come to adore were gone...dead, runaways, or returned to distant families. It was almost too much to bear at times, and Dave found himself trying to distance himself from getting involved with the children, knowing all too well that deep love too often leads to deep pain. In a futile effort to protect himself, Dave would put up an emotional wall only to have it quickly crumble as a small Indian child sneaked up behind him to slip his tiny brown hand into Dave's strong white one.

Each trip was a little different, yet the same thread connected them all—sharing the gospel message of hope that only Jesus promises to a people entrenched in the ancient worship of false gods. Besides spending much time at the REACH Home in Bapatla on India's east coast, various teams also ministered at leper colonies as well as helping rebuild cardboard-box homes in horrendous slums. Following the monstrous December 2004 tsunami that devastated that part of the world, the Life Promotions team worked alongside surviving villagers whose lives were shattered to provide food and begin the enormous job of cleaning up and starting over. Indian lives were changed, no doubt, by the help the teams provided, but even more so the lives of those mission team members and their leaders, Dave and Jen.

India was one of God's many tools for equipping the Bells. The excruciating lessons of learning to love completely despite the risks would be necessary heart-conditioning that would help them survive the years to come. Dave and Jen would learn to never count on tomorrow, to use each moment to its fullest to bring God's love to whatever lives He allowed them to touch.

Each February a trip to the Dominican Republic was on the Bells' mission agenda. The Dominican culture seemed almost communal by American standards. Every door was open and people passed in and out of each others' homes as they pleased, with no privacy nor sense of personal belongings. And the noise! Huge speakers blasted music in the streets until the wee hours of the morning, making sleep impossible even as the teams tried to muffle the sound with pillows over their heads. Then, after finally getting a few hours of sleep, desiring to beat the midday heat and humidity, Dave and Jen and the team would get up early and begin working. It was a strategy the Dominicans did not seem to grasp, preferring to sleep in late, work a couple of hours, eat a meager meal, then take a siesta. Definitely not the work ethic to which the Americans were accustomed!

Dave's niece Karen Miller was living in the Dominican Republic at the time, serving as a missionary teaching English to the villagers while sharing with them about Jesus. Dave and Jen worked closely with Karen's pastor friend Natanel Razon in Azua and its surrounding villages. A new project for the Bells' Life Promotions mission teams was donating the PUR water purifiers to villagers and training them on their use. Unclean water was the source of many health problems in these villages, and clean safe water to drink, which Americans take for granted, was a luxury for those in developing nations such as the Dominican Republic.

One trip started out in a particularly memorable way. Arriving in Santo Domingo late one evening and loading into vans to begin the few-hour drive to Azua, the team got partway there when one of the vans broke down in the middle of nowhere leaving them stranded in the dark, midnight jungle. As they nervously awaited a mechanic to be located and brought to work on the van, the team noticed a small outcrop of buildings tucked into the thick foliage. And on the rooftops of those buildings several men wielding shotguns were keeping wary eyes on the befuddled group of gringos below. Never had a group been so thankful to see a mechanic and more eager to be on their way!

Summers at Life Promotions, Dave oversaw a group of volunteers called the Green Team who handled all the maintenance and grounds responsibilities at the annual July Lifest. This group of incredible servants, who had become close friends and supporters of Dave's over the years, had the goal of building a church during their week in the DR. They quickly learned that building even the most basic structure in the Dominican Republic brought many unforeseen challenges. Simple trips to the hardware store for purchasing supplies were not simple at all. Unlike in the States where one browses through the store, finds what he needs, and gets in a check-out line to pay, it wasn't that easy in the DR. Just finding what they were looking for was challenging enough, as the stores were unorganized stacks of boxes chaotically scattered all over the place without thought to content. Add to that the language barrier, and it quickly became obvious just how little conversational Spanish the team knew and how little, if any, English the shopkeepers understood. The team relied on their crude art skills, drawing pictures to communicate to the shop owner exactly what they were needing. Waiting patiently for their turn at the counter, it soon became apparent that shopping was done differently here. Had they not elbowed their way to the counter they would still be standing there in line! Eventually the shopkeeper would see them coming and just open the storeroom doors, allowing them to wander around until they found what they needed. Or at least something close enough. Undoubtedly the team of gringos provided fodder for much entertainment as those shopkeepers surely told tales about those strange American men to their beer buddies. Despite the frustrating hurdles, the Green Team did finish the church and a part of this group continued their annual trips to Azua long after Dave and Jen quit leading them.

The annual arrival of the Americans was cause for great celebration in the village. They would block off the streets and the whole village would gather to watch the "Jesus" film and hear testimonies from team members. Make-shift Vacation Bible Schools would teach and entertain both children and adults. For poverty-stricken villagers with little to celebrate, the few days with the Americans was the highlight of their year and called for a festival atmosphere with singing and games and laughter and most of all sharing God's love with a desperate people. The Bells and their teams spent time ministering and teaching in Haitian refugee camps and sugar cane camps where living conditions were deplorable and people were starving for the Good News. And each trip brought a visit back to the rehab center the Bells had visited their first time, or going to the Respite Center, a home for youth who had gotten in trouble with the law. So much need, so many desperate lives at stake!

And then there was Rancho Sordo Mudo each March, often with additional trips sprinkled in throughout the year. Some years found Dave and Jen leading back-to-back teams of young people, often spending their college Spring Break serving, dropping off one team at the San Diego airport at the end of a fruitful week only to pick up a new group of volunteers at the same time. This was one of the Bells' favorite places to minister. Spending so many hours in the same place, the Americans forged a strong friendship with the RSM Director Luke Everett. Luke was great inspiration for the Bells and they were wonderful encouragement for him. Running the school in such a desolate location had many challenges and over the years Luke had dealt with much adversity, overcoming obstacles that would have driven most people to the point of collapse and surrender. Not Luke. Dave worked alongside Luke learning how to fix and build things with minimal tools and supplies, how to get creative in his thinking and design when facing seemingly impossible tasks. He also learned very valuable smuggling techniques necessary to get what they needed across the border.

While all of these practical lessons would pay off down the road, the most valuable lesson of all was how it opened the eyes and hearts of both the Bells and their team members to a very different culture, not so very far away geographically, but light years distant in many other ways. The deaf children at the ranch may not have had the gift of hearing like most people did, but they were completely normal in every other way and not "crazy" as the Mexican culture was prone to believe. Teams learned to serve without the many luxury resources they were accustomed to in the States, discovering that God's Word in their hands and hearts was sufficient and provided everything they needed to make an impact on these young lives. Several team members built such strong connections and ties of the heart that they eventually became actual staff members at Rancho Sordo Mudo, serving long after Dave and Jen had stopped leading teams.

April, May, and June were spent, for the most part, making preparations for the Life Promotions summer events: Lifest in mid-July and Hopefest in late July. Lifest especially was a huge undertaking that required lots of planning and organizing, and despite the long hours of work involved was the highlight of each summer for Dave, Jen, Nate, and Chris, who would join them on his summer college breaks.

Autumns brought opportunities for additional trips to Mexico, visits home to Indiana family, planning for the Christmas Day outreach in inner city Milwaukee, as well as making preparations for upcoming international trips in the new year. The Bells' schedule was hectic at times, but they thrived on sharing God's love and truth to searching youth, poverty-stricken families, and those overseas who had never heard the gospel message.

But all this time that God was continuing to fine-tune and equip the Bells, He was also nagging at their hearts. Just subtly at first, but over time the nagging became stronger and both Dave and Jen felt God was calling them away from their comfortable schedule to a new challenge, something long-term that would make a lasting impact on lives. While the short-term trips were wonderful and much good was accomplished, the Bells often thought that those benefiting most from the trips were the American teams who gained new insights and perspectives of the world. Those were definitely worthwhile results, but so often Dave and Jen couldn't help but feel that their trips to the villages were but a small temporary splash in a bucket of need, that they may have stirred the water for a short time, but after they left, the bucket was still left pretty much unchanged. They felt an undeniable pull to something more permanent, ministry opportunities that would ultimately change people's lives. Just where He was calling them, they weren't yet sure. But He had definitely been equipping them for a big new step of faith.

CHAPTER 13

TIK ("This is Kenya")

April 2006

Just in the nick of time, Dave's tongue darted out and snatched the sweet drop. Lost in deep thoughts and pondering the future of his family, Dave had momentarily forgotten the ice cream cone he was holding in his hand, its frozen sweetness slowly melting despite the chilly Wisconsin autumn air.

Quickly he licked the creamy mound as he turned the cone, trying to get the deliciousness back under control. Lick and turn. The irony was not lost on Dave, as his mind flashed back to the simple childhood life lesson his Dad Myron had taught him forty years before. Lick and turn. That advice applied to much more than ice cream. As he and Jen faced this major crossroad in their life, those three words were more pertinent than ever.

Bundled against the cool October breeze, Dave and Jen smiled at each other across the table outside the Neenah, Wisconsin Dairy Queen. Nearly eight hours before, they had left Nate home doing school work and they'd made the drive into Neenah to pray and talk and decide. And they'd done just that. Over two meals and a few ice cream treats sitting right there on that concrete bench outside DQ, they'd hashed over every thought, every concern, every angle, every perspective. And God had led them both to the same conviction.

Dave, Jen, and Nate were going to move to Kenya.

Doing exactly what, they weren't sure. God hadn't clearly revealed that yet. One step at a time…

Ever since their recent return from their second trip to Kenya, they knew. Deep in their bones, they both felt clearly the call of their Lord to move to Kenya. On the plane ride home and over the past several days both together and individually they had prayed, talked, prayed some more, agonized, fasted, wondered, and then prayed even harder. Discussing the possibility with Nate, he had been praying too. It was a life-changing decision for the entire family. All three were of one mind: God was calling them to Kenya and they would obey.

Life Promotions Director Bob Lenz graciously received the news. He hated losing them on his staff, for sure. Dave and Jen had filled the roles of Building Manager and Office Manager as well as Lifest staff for several years now. Their leaving would create some major staffing holes to fill. Yet when the Bells shared their heart and what they believed God was calling them to do, Bob was very excited for them and confirmed their calling to move into full-time mission service. He suggested they continue using Life Promotions as their sending agency, and so under their non-profit umbrella Dave and Jen would become Life Missionaries. Through a few tearful hugs, it meant a great deal to the Bells that Bob gave them his blessing.

Following their final Life Promotions event, the Power of One that November, Dave, Jen, and Nate went to Indiana for a couple of weeks. First they went to see Chris, who was living in an apartment in Anderson, attending Anderson University, and working at the Madison County Youth Center, all the while planning for his June 2006 wedding to Ariel. Even though his immediate life wouldn't be impacted as much as Nate's, it would be a life-changer for Chris too, having his family 8000 miles away. But Chris, like Nate, knew the passion in Dave and Jen's hearts and understood that when God calls his parents would obey. Goodness knows, he'd seen that obedience in action countless times in his lifetime!

Next Dave and Jen visited their parents and families, sharing their decision. While those were difficult meetings with a few tears and lots of questions, Dave's folks Myron and Phyllis as well as Jen's dad Earl all gave their blessings. As tough as the news was for them to hear and process, deep in their hearts they understood. They would miss their children, that's for certain, but they wanted more than anything for Dave and Jen to be in the center of God's will for their lives.

Extended family and friends understandably had mixed reactions. Dave and Jen answered questions as best they could, but even they were not sure of many things. Where would they live long-term, exactly what would they be doing, what about finances, how safe was it, and the biggest question: why? Dave and Jen had to admit they didn't have satisfactory responses for most of those questions, but the "why" one they were confident they DID know the answer. God was leading them to Kenya and they were obediently following. And that was all they needed.

December of 2005 through March of 2006 found the Bells preparing for the biggest move of their lives. Splitting time between Wisconsin and Indiana, there were so many things to take care of before leaving: getting rid of/donating unnecessary items they had accumulated over the past few years, visiting family and friends, raising funds for their new venture, making connections in Kenya so they would have a starting line once they arrived, and tying up loose ends at Life Promotions to ensure a smooth transition when they left.

Then in April 2006, Dave, Jen, and Nate cleaned out the Sonshine Housing apartment they had called home for the past four years, boxed up what little they had for temporarily storage in the garage and basement of their close Indiana friends Tom and Amy Roberts, packed eleven bags of clothes and basic supplies, and flew out of Dayton, Ohio, into the unknown.

Twenty-four hours later, William, the driver for HEART, the mission organization through which the Bells would be serving, picked them up at the Nairobi, Kenya airport. HEART is an anacronym for

Health Education Africa Resource Team, and on both their previous trips to Kenya they had used the HEART compound as their home base. Dave and Jen had learned much about the HEART ministry while staying there and the HEART directors had invited them to join their ministry. The Bells heartily agreed and felt that, even if it wasn't to be their permanent station, HEART would be a great launching pad for their Kenyan service. The HEART compound was an old safari lodge with multiple buildings, and the Bells would move into a large house on the compound.

Just a few minutes into the drive from the Nairobi airport to the HEART compound, Dave, Jen, and Nate, who by this time thought they'd surely "seen it all" in their numerous stays in developing countries, were appalled and hit suddenly with the realization that they were NOT in Wisconsin anymore. Driving out of Nairobi, William swerved around a dead body lying in the middle of the major highway going into the city. A DEAD HUMAN BODY! This Kenyan man never even flinched, just quickly steered the van around the uncovered, mangled corpse and kept right on going! As they stopped at two police check points on their way to the HEART compound, Dave's mind went where it hadn't before, realizing that he would soon be behind a steering wheel himself in this traffic craziness. Wordlessly looking at each other, all three Bells were wondering what they (and God!) had gotten into!

In God's wisdom, He had not yet revealed many things about the Kenyan culture that the Bells would learn in the coming weeks. Travel in itself was an adventure not for the faint-hearted, as even short trips were difficult. Pot holes big enough to swallow a car, speed bumps that were more like speed hills, and security checkpoints made a dash to the grocery into a half-day trauma. Dodging the reckless massive trucks hauling who-knows-what, jolting and bouncing their way past broken-down vehicles just abandoned where they died, and crashed matatus (cram-packed, brightly-painted, and music-blaring privately-owned mini buses transporting Kenyans) lying on their sides in the ditches made Dave and Jen very thankful for the unseen angels that surely must be protecting them. The Bells quickly learned to cover every trip, no matter how seemingly insignificant, with prayer.

Learning to maneuver the traffic issues wasn't the only challenge the Bells faced. Many things about the Kenyan culture puzzled even these seasoned travelers, and over the next weeks, months, and even years they would continue to learn lessons, often hard ones, about life in Kenya. Dave would often say, "TIK,"…"This is Kenya." It seemed to be explanation enough for many of the otherwise unexplainable and illogical situations they faced daily.

One of the big lessons that had to be learned, and relearned again and yet again, was the cultural tendency of a Kenyan to tell someone what he thinks the other person, especially if that other person is a mzungu, wants to hear. Even if it is not the truth. For Dave, who valued honesty and integrity as honorable traits in a man, this was difficult to understand.

Time has little importance for a Kenyan. It was a rare event the Bells attended that actually began at the appointed time. A wedding that was supposed to start at 2:00 p.m. may not have begun until after 5:00. Dave learned that when he was invited to preach at a church, it was not the right question to ask "what time does the service start?" The right question was "what time will I need to be there to preach?" It is not uncommon for a service to start with two or three hours of worship with music. Meetings would begin once everyone was there. Even if that was two hours late. The Bells were often told that Kenyans have time, but Americans have watches. A good bit of wisdom, yet a hard lesson for time-conscious Americans to accept.

Dealing with corruption at every level was also a new challenge for the Bells. Much of the Kenyan work force, at least the 40% or so that were actually employed, were typically very much underpaid, so it was understandable why so many asked for a bribe or a "bit of chai tea" for any kind of help. While getting stopped at a police checkpoint was pretty common, the most frustrating part would be when the officer trumped up a charge and then was willing to let them go if Dave gave him a little "something."

Dealing with all of these challenges was worthwhile because of the people, the wonderful Kenyan people with whom Dave and Jen had fallen in love, the vast majority of them living in spiritual darkness, scores dying every single day from the devastating AIDS epidemic while others not yet experiencing full-blown AIDS but still HIV+ being shunned and rejected by not only society but even their families. Having seen lepers in India suffer the same kind of agonizing shunning from those who should love them most, Dave and Jen recognized that God had used their willingness to have physical contact with those lepers to prepare them for their work in Kenya with AIDS victims.

But what pulled most at the heartstrings of the Bells were the children, innocent casualties of the AIDS infestation. No family was untouched by the devastation, indeed an entire generation seemed to be in danger of extinction, leaving behind desperate grandparents in ill health with measly resources and barely surviving themselves to feed hungry mouths and care for toddlers. Overwhelmed by the impossible circumstances, many children were abandoned to fend for themselves. It was these precious ones, God's least of these, that drew the Bells to Kenya.

The AIDS epidemic seemed so hopeless, so out-of-control, like a massive tsunami moving through the African continent. While not every Kenyan was infected, all were affected, no family left untouched by its ruthless assault. The need was so great, the decimation so incomprehensible that the Bells and other missionaries felt helpless against its staggering assault. No matter how hard they tried, their efforts would be a mere drop in the ocean of despair and suffering. Dave and Jen would often compare it the story of the stranded starfish, tens of thousands of them washed ashore after a terrible storm and sure to die outside of their sea home. A little child walking along the beach picked them up, one by one, tossing them back into the ocean. When questioned about the impossibility of the enormous task, that he could never make a difference, the young yet wise child answered. Perhaps he couldn't save them all, but he could make a difference to those few, one at a time.

This starfish philosophy came to define Dave and Jen's life work for God in Kenya. No, the reality was that they couldn't make a huge difference in the overall scheme of the devastating situation, but they would and could make a huge difference in the lives of those that God placed in their paths.

And so it was that in April 2006, Dave, Jen, and Nate Bell began their new lives in Kenya, Life Missionaries under the wings of Life Promotions living at the HEART compound and working alongside the HEART missionaries doing outreaches in villages all across Kenya and in the slums of Nairobi.

Along with the constant of sharing the gospel everywhere they went, one of the main focuses of the Bells was educating Kenyan people on the facts about HIV/AIDS and teaching youth the importance of maintaining sexual purity until marriage, information sorely lacking and desperately needed if there was to be any halting of the steam-rolling AIDS crisis. Soon after arriving in Kenya, Dave, Jen, and Nate visited the remote village of Ndumbini where they had their first African overnight camping experience. The whole village turned out for the teaching of the Bells and their HEART colleagues, people of all ages and genders squeezed together to be able to hear the teaching, hungry and thirsty to learn. The missionaries feared the village elders might feel threatened and stop the teaching, but God had other plans and many youth that day chose to make a pledge of purity. God was already answering prayers.

They began making connections with the area children's homes of which there were sadly but necessarily many. Each visit brought a mixture of joyful laughter and sad tears as Dave and Jen interacted with the precious children there, each one with his/her heartbreaking story. Unspeakably horrible circumstances so many had lived through, like little six-year-old Edna, an AIDS orphan who had been rescued off the street. She had been brutally raped, so physically damaged that surgery was needed to repair her little body. Only God, Jen knew, could repair the emotional damage that no one could see. So many Ednas out there, so much evil.

Satan had a powerful foothold in Kenya, a literal death grip on the country, his evil fingers dug in deeply, using the AIDS epidemic, barbaric cultural traditions, apathy, corruption, and poverty to destroy the Kenyan people from within. It was overwhelming at times and Dave and Jen often went to bed at night discouraged and beaten down, but even from the beginning, God showed them small victories and proofs that they were making a difference. One life at a time.

Each new day those first few months brought new lessons, new challenges to be met. And soon after getting settled into their new home, Dave and Jen began hosting short-term mission teams through Life Promotions, sharing these experiences with them.

Jen's first Mother's Day in Kenya was a memorable one, one that would eventually impact her entire life. They visited an infant rescue center called New Life, a home that took in and cared for abandoned babies. Not placing the same value on life that much of the world does, unwanted infants are often viewed as disposable, left lying on streets or in the bush. The rationale varies; perhaps an unwed mother is shunned by her village, maybe the child has an abnormality that the culture considers to be a curse upon the family, sometimes the babe is the product of incest, a strong taboo in the Kenyan culture. But very often AIDS plays heavily into the abandonment, as many young women giving birth are stricken with AIDS and struggling to live. So these tiniest of victims, innocent babies, are left to die.

That day Jen's eyes and heart were opened wide to this huge catastrophe of infant abandonment, and a passion was ignited deep inside her that would never be extinguished. New Life was caring for more than 50 infants at that time, from a two-pound one-week-old preemie to 2 ½-year-old toddlers. Arriving at New Life just at feeding time, Dave and Jen and the rest of the HEART team were handed infants and bottles of formula to feed them. Nestling a little one against her, Jen melted as she kissed, sang to, prayed over, and loved on this greatest of God's gifts, a new life. Not so unlike the joy she had felt as a little girl caring for her daddy's abandoned runt baby pigs, but these new lives were so much more important in God's Kingdom. The Bells felt honored just to play a tiny role in saving them. That experience at New Life that Mother's Day impacted them all in ways they had no inkling of at the time. But God knew....

Then there were the slums.

One of two major Nairobi slums, the Mathare slum was home to an estimated 500,000 people. Over two-thirds of the slum-dwellers were under the age of fourteen, with at least 100,000 of those orphans due to the 40% HIV/AIDS infection rate. In the Mathare slums, a person died every ten minutes. It truly was hell on earth.

A few high-rise buildings dotted the landscape, but they made American ghettos look like luxury housing. No electricity, no water, no moving air in the stifling, stomach-turning heat. Trash and raw sewage were everywhere, and the only green in the entire slum were the few stubborn blades of grass along the polluted Mathare River. The garbage-lined river was their only water supply, itself reeking of death and decay. Naked children bathing, women scrubbing rags of clothing on its rocks, others filling water jugs to carry back to their metal and cardboard homes for drinking and cooking.

Thousands of those homes propped up side by side, a never-ending line of rusty metal and fraying cardboard, made up the slums. Living inside these eight-foot-square makeshift shelters were extended families of eight to ten people sharing two "rooms" separated by a sheet hanging from a piece of suspended twine. Gullies had been dug between every cluster of shacks, all dribbling urine, excrement, and waste water down towards the river, which had long been choked by every sordid refuse that mankind can create.

But even in the midst of this wretched place there were glimmers of light, like the WEEP (Women Equality Empowerment

Project) Center, so named because the founder of HEART could hear in her heart the HIV widows crying out for their children. When one of the women asked why it was named WEEP and she explained, several of the Kenyan mothers whispered to her, "It was me you heard crying."

At the Mathare WEEP Center, there were ten women at the time, all widowed mothers who were HIV+, all basically facing a death sentence with no hope of living long enough to see their children grow up. That is, until WEEP. Not only had they been given new physical hope by receiving life-extending ARVs (anti-retroviral vaccines), drugs which had literally brought them back from the brink of death, but they also learned how to sew on the treadle sewing machines provided by HEART allowing them to earn enough money to provide for their children. But even more important than hope for survival was the hope they had received learning about the life-saving love of Jesus through the missionaries there.

Another glimmer of light shining in the Mathare slum darkness was a group of seventeen young men and women who grew up in the slums but had found salvation in Jesus and were working to help change the lives of fellow slum-dwellers. Knowing first-hand the suffering and obstacles their neighbors faced daily, they were reaching out to their neighbors in practical ways as the hands of Christ. Instead of moving out of the slums and bettering their lives, these incredible servants chose to remain there and care for these people that society had forgotten.

And then there were the children who were just like any children any other place on the globe, despite the destitution of the only life they had ever known. Running, laughing, smiling, playing in the mud, faces of joy despite the raggedy clothes, scabies sores covering their little bodies. It was difficult for Dave and Jen and their American mission teams not to cringe as dirty fingers grabbed at the mzungus again and again as they made their way through the slums, yelling out to them in one of the only English phrases they knew "How are you? How are you?" and touching their white arms, fascinated by the color and hair on them. Knowing that any affection those precious children received from their American visitors would likely be the only love shown to them that day, Dave and Jen would bend down and love on these forgotten little souls.

It was in Mathare that God showed Dave how his years of straying from the Lord could be used in the right situation. Deep in the bowels of Mathare sat a "moonshine" still. The men that operated it brewed changaa, the Kenyan version of moonshine. Hundreds of people died or went blind each year when a batch was made incorrectly and turned out to be poisonous to drink.

After several months of teaching and loving in the slums, word came to Dave that the leader of this group wanted to meet him. He had heard of Dave's testimony about his misuse of alcohol. Dave, who was told he was the first white man to be invited there, agreed to meet this gentleman at a community building so he could lead him to the still.

Before they even arrived at the still, the odor hit Dave's nostrils, the sickenly-sweet smell of the mash as it was being cooked. Soon the still came into sight, a jumble of rusty coils running down into the sewage-filled Mathare River used to cool the liquid.

But the biggest impression was left by the men who did the brewing and drinking of the changaa. Their hollowed dark eyes filled with looks of hopelessness struck a familiar chord with Dave. Over the coming months, Dave had several opportunities to share the Gospel and its message of hope with these desperate men. And while none made a confession of faith to Dave, it was clear that God was working in their hearts and minds, and Dave clung to the promise that God's Word never comes back void.

Even in the hell hole that was Mathare, God was there. These abandoned people, much like the lepers and Untouchables in India, truly were some of "the least of these" that Jesus spoke about in Matthew 25: 40, *"I tell you the truth, whatever you did for one of the least of these brothers of mine, you did for me."* Over the many trips to Mathare, Dave and Jen would meet many remarkable people stuck living there, yet incredibly joyful despite their circumstances because of the salvation they found in Jesus and that this place was only their temporary home, their eternal Home being in Heaven. Hope. Even in Mathare there was hope.

Those first few months living in Kenya, Dave and Jen's eyes were opened to new things every day. Many of those situations brought feelings of frustration, aggravation, and bewilderment but there were also many light-hearted moments along the way. God knew they needed a good laugh every now and then!

One such incident happened that first summer in their HEART ministry, when Dave, Jen, Nate, and two women on a short-term mission team traveled to the village of Kibwezi. Arriving at the house where they would be staying for a couple of days, Dave went to check the choo, Swahili for "toilet," to make sure it was usable for the gals. He noticed a few cockroaches around it, so he took a can of Doom bug spray, a staple for the Bells, liberally sprayed it into the hole, and walked out feeling like a knight in shining armor. A few moments later, one of the women went in to use the choo and ran out screaming like a banshee! A wave of thousands upon thousands of cockroaches were flowing out from under the choo door. The bug spray had apparently forced them all out, and there were so many that the Americans could hear them running across the metal roof of the house, trying to escape. The bug spray eventually killed them, but not quite fast enough!

To make the toilet incident even more exciting, the banquet of cockroaches brought the scorpions out from their hiding places. The team danced around, crunching any moving critter they could stomp on. When the lady of the house, to whom the Bells never had the opportunity to speak, was sweeping up large piles of dead cockroaches and scorpions the next morning, she surely must have wondered what in tarnation those weird wazungus (white people) had done.

In the midst of all the horrors of the manmade messes they found in Kenya, God provided a respite of sorts. One of the responsibilities that fell on the Bells was to take teams on safari during their time in Kenya. The Bells quickly fell in love with the beauty of Tsavo West Park in South East Kenya. The 3,500-square-mile park was home to the beauty of extinct volcanoes and open savannahs that were breathtaking. While Dave had always dreamed of going on a big game hunt in Africa, that desire was somewhat quenched by the frequent opportunities they had to watch elephants, hippo, giraffe, zebra, and more.

Many priceless memories were created on those safari drives. Watching the beauty of what God created in the animals cannot be done justice with the best of cameras. And nothing gets one's heart pounding quite like the thrill of being chased by a ten-foot tall, 10,000-pound bull elephant!

The American teams the Bells brought even caused the administration to make some changes at Kilaguni Lodge where they stayed. Since most of its clientele was either Asian or European, neither of which use much ice, getting a glass of ice was a bit of a challenge. After several visits, the lodge manager came up to Dave with a big smile and informed him that they now had an ice machine. And over the years it has certainly gotten a workout!

As much as the park itself impressed the Bells, it was the staff at Kilaguni Lodge that they loved most. It was as if God had prepared them to minister to the Bells each time they visited the lodge. Over the years the Bells visited many of the staff's rural villages and homes to conduct teachings on health and farming. The strong relationships the Bells and the staff developed continues even now, with each trip to Kilaguni like a homecoming.

Major culture shock for Dave, Jen, and Nate those beginning months, definitely a time of transition. Slowly but surely the family became somewhat acclimated to their new home, life in Kenya becoming more comfortable all the time. Their new normal.

TIK.

CHAPTER 14

Angels All Around

October 2, 2006

Nairobi, Kenya

The scream began silently, conceived down in the deepest part of Dave's very core, a voiceless primal scream of terror that momentarily paralyzed him. For those few horrific seconds, time seemed to stop. A bone-crushing jolt, the tinkling of shattering glass, the shrill screeching of crumpling metal, the world whirling around him in surreal slow motion as if in a nightmare. Then silence, a split second of total eerie silence before the moans and cries pierced the stillness and shook Dave back to stunned reality.

Beside Dave, in the passenger's seat, his friend violently convulsed and Dave frantically wondered if he might be suffering from a heart attack. In the back seat...behind him...Dave was afraid to even look behind him....

The Monday morning of October 2, 2006 began, as most mornings did in the Bells' house at the HEART compound, with family devotions. That morning God had placed the song "Rock of Ages" and Psalm 61 on their hearts.

"O God, listen to me! Hear my prayer.
For wherever I am, though far away at the ends of the earth,
I will cry to you for help.

When my heart is faint and overwhelmed,
lead me to the mighty towering Rock of safety."
Psalm 61: 1-2, The Living Bible

Thanking God in prayer for being their Rock and vowing to praise Him every day, little did they know how they would hang onto those very words and prayer before the day was through.

That evening had begun relatively carefree for the Bells, their close friends the Puringtons, and another missionary couple living at the HEART compound. A frequent annoyance in Kenya, the power had gone out just when the three families were beginning to prepare dinner. They had had plans for a relaxed evening in the compound, as there were no teams to care for and the work for the day finished. A nice meal and a quiet evening of rest was their only agenda. But with no way to cook their evening meal, the friends decided to splurge on a rare dinner out together. Mark and Camille Purington went on ahead in their car with plans for the Dave, Jen, Nate, and the others to join them for dinner at the Java House on the north side of Nairobi.

Climbing into the white Toyota Corolla station wagon that belonged to HEART, the five friends buckled into the seats, chatting and laughing. Dave got behind the steering wheel, (per British standards, on the right side of the car), with his friend and his friend's wife on the passenger side, he in the front passenger seat and she behind him. Jen crawled into the middle rear seat and Nate folded his long legs up to sit by the window behind his dad. Nate would have preferred to ride, as he often did, in the back luggage area where he had much more room for his six-foot frame, but Dave and Jen insisted this particular time that he squeeze into the seat and buckle up, so Nate had quietly obliged his parents' request. Traveling down the busy two-lane highway, (again, per British standards, on the left side of the road), the group was enjoying a rare night of freedom and even the always-frustrating traffic wasn't dampening their spirits.

Daylight was fading and the group found their low-riding station wagon stuck behind a big truck. Needing to make a right-hand turn across traffic, Dave nosed the station wagon out to be able to see before turning. No on-coming traffic in sight, he began pulling across the highway when a large SUV came over the hill out of nowhere, hurtling at a high rate of speed right toward their vehicle. Later investigation would bring to light that the driver of the SUV was frustrated after just having been detained at a checkpoint, leading to him recklessly driving at an estimated 90 mph.

The speeding SUV t-boned the Corolla, crashing squarely between the two car doors on the passenger side. The forceful impact spun the station wagon into the air and around several times as the SUV flipped over the top of it, and both came to rest several yards apart in the ditch along the highway.

A split second of eerie silence was soon broken by the convulsions of his friend beside him and low groans of agony from the back seat. Stunned but relatively okay physically, when Dave dared look over his left shoulder he quickly realized that all three passengers in the back seat were in bad shape. The lady was conscious and moaning, but covered with blood. Nate's face was bloodied and he was yelling. And Jen. Jen was unconscious and not moving.

Frantic with fear, Dave's fingers fumbled in his silent hysteria, but finally he managed to unbuckle his seat belt and pull himself out of the mangled car. He opened Nate's door behind him and helped his son, who was bloody and scared but otherwise seemed not to be seriously injured, out of the car. Climbing across the seat to get to Jen, Dave immediately could see she wasn't breathing. Struggling to frantically unbuckle her, to no avail Dave screamed her name and willed her to respond. His heart seizing with terror at the thought of losing his bride, Dave dragged her limp body out of the car and laid her in the grass. Just as he was about to start CPR on her, Jen took a small gasp and began breathing again on her own, and Dave silently praised God. Jen was still alive, hurt badly, but still alive.

Onlookers began slowing and stopping, but no one was eager to step forward and help. Dave knelt on the grass beside Jen, holding her hand and trying to get her to respond, struggling to make sense of her incoherent mumblings. Finally he was able to make out the word "back," Jen was trying to say something about her back. It was then that Dave realized that in his haste to get her out of the car and breathing, he had tugged her body across the seat without thinking about her back. Perhaps he himself had further injured her! The thought itself terrified him even more.

Just then, Dave looked up to see a black man who identified himself as a doctor kneeling beside them. As Jen continued mumbling about her back, the doctor checked her and Dave let out a sigh of relief as the doctor told him her back was not severely injured but she had internal trauma and needed to get to a hospital right away, specifically the Aga Khan Hospital. After he finished speaking and began to rise, Dave glanced back at Jen for a second before turning to thank the doctor for his help. He was gone, disappearing in the blink of an eye.

Later, replaying the events of the evening with the others involved, Dave told them about the doctor who helped. The others looked back and forth at each other with puzzled eyes. No one else had seen him. Even Nate, who had been standing right next to his dad and mom, did not see the doctor. Only Dave had seen him, had watched him examine Jen, had heard him speak reassuringly and decisively. Dave would forever maintain that this "invisible doctor" was an angel of the Lord.

As Dave sat on the grass beside Jen, puzzled by the sudden appearance and disappearance of the doctor, a few vehicles began to stop and offer help. Dave, still in shock but slowly coming to his senses, phoned Dr. Meshach Onguti who was a personal family friend with a strong affiliation with HEART. Meshach initially told Dave to have Jen taken to a big hospital in Nairobi, then knowing it would be at least an hour's drive there he reconsidered and told Dave to instead take her to Aga Khan Hospital. Having driven past Aga Khan many times, Dave knew where it was but had always assumed it to be a Hindu or Muslim hospital. But trusting his friend's advice and remembering the recommendation of the "doctor," when a kind Kenyan lady named Faith driving a little two-door car volunteered to drive them to the nearest hospital, Dave accepted her generous offer. Knowing that in Kenya an ambulance would probably take hours to arrive, Dave picked up and carried Jen, placing her in the reclined passenger seat of the tiny car, and squeezed in beside her. There was no room for anyone else, and sixteen-year-old Nate insisted they go on without him, that he would get a ride. So Dave and Jen headed to the hospital, leaving their son standing beside the crashed Corolla.

Meanwhile, other vehicles stopped to take the other injured people to the hospital as well. An American family happened upon the crash scene and, seeing Nate sitting there all alone, stayed with him until Mark and Camille, who Dave called en route to the hospital, circled back to pick him up.

All the way to the hospital, Jen passionately cried out to Jesus, non-stop fervently and vocally praying, confessing Jesus as her Lord and Savior even through her pain. Her witness made quite an impact on Faith, as a few days afterward she would write them a note sharing how it "challenged" her as she drove. Faith was so convicted and affected by Jen's unconscious testimony that she told her pastor about it and he even put together a sermon around that theme, entitled "What Comes Out When God Squeezes You?" Jen would later say she was passed out during that time and had no memory of the wreck or the ride to the hospital. Jen may not have remembered it, but God was at work even then.

What Jen did remember was waking up in the emergency room in excruciating pain and nauseous. She had no idea where she was or how she had gotten there, but she was hurting. Badly. Nate was there with her, along with their friends Mark and Camille, who had picked Nate up from the accident scene. As the doctor came in to examine her,

Jen adamantly refused to let anyone touch her until they had prayed! And so Nate did, praying for his mother and the doctors right then and there. Over the next few days, Nate continued to be very protective of Jen, hovering over her and making sure no one caused her pain moving her around for tests and x-rays. Dave was very, very proud of his sixteen-year-old son who proved himself a man during the terrible ordeal.

Dave was not in Jen's room when she woke up. He was bouncing between rooms, trying to be sure everyone was receiving care. Moving back and forth through the hospital's emergency room, he noticed the injured driver of the SUV that had hit them still waiting for treatment in the ER. When the Bells' friend Dr. Onguti met them at the hospital, they discovered that he knew the brother of the driver of the SUV. In a Kenyan emergency room, medical treatment is not given until payment is made. This man, who obviously was in terrible pain himself with a severely broken arm, might sit there for hours until someone came and paid the hospital. Fighting his own feelings about the accident, Dave insisted the man be seen right away and paid the 60,000 ksh (Kenyan shillings, about $600 USD) to make it happen.

After everyone was finally being treated, the reality of injuries began to set in. Dave, being furthest from the point of impact, suffered assorted bruises and a great deal of soreness. Nate had chipped a tooth as his mouth collided with Jen's head, and was bruised all over. The other three were admitted to the hospital. All sustained internal organ trauma with several broken bones and cuts, but thankfully none of their injuries were life-threatening.

Jen had been sitting in the middle back seat. Her injuries, besides the gash on her head where Nate had chipped his tooth, were a fractured pelvis, two cracked ribs, and a broken left shoulder. Doctors anticipated up to six weeks for recovery, perhaps half of those spent in the hospital.

Three days later Dave went to the police station to fill out the accident report, which had not yet been done, again, TIK... Not far from Dave's mind were the many horror stories he had heard about Americans being jailed after an accident with the intent of receiving a large bribe to settle things. The police station was a ten-by-ten-foot wooden shack, makeshift shelves stacked precariously high with dusty old records. Sitting on a wooden bench, Dave recounted the accident and gave his statement as the officer wrote it down, interrupted several times by passers-through and others he was dealing with at the same time. Although it took two long hours for him to fill out a three-page statement, the officer was very friendly and kind, asking what they were doing in Kenya and even expressing an interest in becoming involved in the ministry. Dave did not take it for granted when he was released without charges. God had his back once again!

It was there at the police station that Dave also got his first look at the cars involved in the collision. If Dave had any doubts before, just seeing the condition of those cars confirmed what he already knew in his heart -- only God's protection that night had sent them to the emergency room instead of the funeral home! The back passenger door was shoved in almost a foot. The hinges had been ripped from the frame, the rear axle broken in two, and the seat belts torn away, thankfully they had done their job the one time they were needed. Across the roof of the Corolla were streaks of paint left as the SUV had slid over. The SUV that had hit them was even worse, completely crushed in on top and both sides as well as the crumpled nose where the impact had happened. Weighing easily twice as much as their little Corolla wagon, only the hand of God and His angels could have flipped that vehicle over the top of them; had it landed on the Toyota, all in both vehicles would surely have been killed. Had they not been buckled in, had Nate been in the luggage area as he so often was...walking around the totaled vehicles, Dave praised God that miraculously all involved had survived.

God always keeps His promises, one of which is found in Romans 8: 28. *"We know that in all things God works for the good of those who love him, who have been called according to his purpose."* Turning bad into good is one of God's specialties, and many blessings came from the horrific accident. Countless medical staff heard the gospel and saw God's peace and love in action as they cared for Jen. Throughout her time in the hospital, Jen's strength and faith was demonstrated over and over again. The nurses bickered over who got to care for her, she was such an inspiration and a beacon of light in a place where there was so much pain. A few days after the accident and before Jen had been allowed out of bed, Dave was concerned when he came to visit to find that she was not in her room, and the nurses that normally were there also were not around. After a few minutes of nervous searching, Dave found them all down the hall, Jen sitting in a borrowed wheelchair and sharing the Gospel with several hospital staff. Even in her suffering Jen ministered to those around her and many hearts were touched.

Since arriving in Kenya, Dave and Jen had been hoping to build a pool of medical professionals, nurses and doctors who were willing to volunteer in the medical camps HEART provided during their health seminars across Kenya. Several nurses would eventually become volunteers as a result of the accident ordeal.

Dave also witnessed to many while at the hospital with Jen. He was grateful for the opportunity to connect one of the hospital staff whose close relative was HIV+ with some fellow Kenyans to encourage him. The encourager turned out to be a long-time friend of this man, the two had grown up together but hadn't seen each other for years. Once more, God was doing healing work, not only of bodies but also of hearts.

Jen's ministry from her hospital bed would continue until her release over three weeks later. Even after going home to the HEART compound, she still had a long road of recovery ahead, requiring much therapy and patience. That October evening became a life-changer for all involved, a terrible experience yet one that left them even more in awe of their Creator. Dave, Jen, and Nate had personally encountered the invisible presence of God's angels around them, an experience for which they would forever be grateful. As painful as it was to walk through that storm, they would come to realize the precious heavenly rewards gained and in retrospect found it was totally worth it. God never wastes experiences, good or bad. Yet another opportunity to savor His goodness…another opportunity to lick and turn.

CHAPTER 15

Winds of Change

December 2007

Kitengela, Kenya

C hange.

Human nature is to resist change. And yet sometimes it seemed the only real constant in the Bells' life since God had called them into full-time missionary work WAS change. God hadn't yet moved them where He wanted them to finally land, and apparently He didn't want them getting too comfortable in any one spot.

Now another big change was upon them. Not only were they moving to Kitengela, a small-town suburb south of Nairobi, but Dave and Jen were now working with a new mission organization, Christ Hope International.

The weeks following the accident were filled with painful rehabilitation for Jen. Eventually her shoulder repair would require three separate surgeries, each one beginning another round of excruciating therapy. Before going into each surgery, Jen insisted upon prayer and would tell the surgeon that while she realized her shoulder would never be the same as before the injury, she needed to be able to hold babies. Determined not to let any roadblocks keep her from her Father's work, as soon as Jen was at all mobile she was joining forces with fellow missionaries from HEART and ministering to anyone who crossed her path, getting back into the swing of life in Kenya as quickly as possible.

The year 2006 had certainly been a monumental year of changes for the Bells. A calling to full-time missionary work. A move overseas. A wedding of their oldest son Chris to Ariel. A near-death experience with the accident. In each and every change, Dave and Jen witnessed the love of God who held them and carried them through each circumstance as only He can. And now as 2006 came to a close and 2007 began, another change was upon them.

Life Promotions, which had sent out their first international missionaries in the persons of the Bells, had decided to shift their focus back to their original avenues of ministry. That meant that Life Missions, Dave and Jen's wing of the ministry, was on the chopping block. Life Promotions would no longer be their sending agency and their funds would no longer go through Life Promotions as before. As the Bells learned of this transition, HEART extended its hand and agreed to take over the role of being Dave and Jen's sending agency as well as managing their resources. Besides a few logistics and growing pains along the way, the Bells' ministry continued much as it had before the switch.

Coordinating and hosting short-term mission teams from the States continued to be a very important part of that ministry. Having reluctantly severed ties with Life Promotions at this point, they were still hosting teams from the Wisconsin area, connections they'd made those years living there. Dave and Jen enjoyed introducing team members who had never stepped outside the USA to a world they never imagined existed.

A world where countless mothers, many terminally-ill with AIDS, fell asleep each night to the sounds of their babies crying because they were hungry. A world where thousands of children somehow survived on their own in the slums, a pile of rotting garbage for their bed. A world where tribal loyalty trumped protecting innocent children from abuse or rape by relatives. A world with such magnitude of physical, emotional, and spiritual suffering that God often seemed very, very far away.

The Bells took teams to various children's homes and villages doing AIDS testing and counseling, providing medical clinics and organizing sports programs, distributing school uniforms and goats to AIDS orphans, providing mosquito bed nets and food supplies to families in villages so remote that some there had never before laid their eyes upon wazungus, sharing the hope of Jesus at every opportunity. Each day was different, yet it soon became apparent that a common heart-thread ran through the gamut of Dave and Jen's ministries: saving children.

God was slowly, deliberately, undoubtedly, subtly fine-tuning His calling on the Bells' life. Looking back years later, it would be easy to see how He was using each experience, each encounter, each heart-breaking situation to mold them for the special ministry into which He would eventually call them. But at the time, of course, they couldn't see the future. All they knew was that little by little, day after day after day they were putting their hearts and souls into making a difference to one life at a time.

Most especially one CHILD at a time.

Along the way, certain children wormed their ways into the Dave, Jen, and Nate's hearts. One such little boy was Victor. The Bells first laid eyes on the little eight-month-old boy during a May 2006 visit to a village called Getumo. During a team visit to teach the health seminar, run HIV testing, do a medical camp, and share the Purity Project with the youth of Getumo, a mother of six brought her youngest child to show the Bells her baby's deformed hand. She was so embarrassed that she kept it covered so others could not see, as any "imperfections" in Kenya are considered curses and bring stigma and shame on the family. Victor's thumb and index finger were enlarged and not functional, and the Bells immediately felt if they could arrange medical intervention soon, Victor's life would be changed forever.

When it was finally worked out several weeks later for the mother to bring Victor to a Nairobi hospital for x-rays and to see a doctor, it was determined that Victor suffered from a form of giantism, and by

Victor   2006

now things had gotten much worse with the entire arm as well as the hand much enlarged. The doctors warned that if surgery wasn't done soon the baby would permanently lose the use of his arm and hand. So the Bells put out a plea to their American partners for donations to raise the $5000 needed for Victor's surgery.

While monies did arrive, time was of the essence and as Victor's hand and arm worsened, only about half of the necessary funds had been raised. But the surgery couldn't wait, somehow they would find the funds. However, as always, God was at work behind the scenes and when the Bells were led to take Victor to CURE Hospital in Kijabe, which was run by a Christian organization that specialized in charitable surgeries for children, they discovered that this hospital would operate on Victor for around $1000. God had provided a way!

Victor's first surgery required removing his thumb and index finger, as well as "debulking" much of his hand and arm to eliminate the extra fat. Several months later Victor would have a second surgery to move one of his three remaining fingers to the thumb position so he would have opposing digits to use. Victor, a big smile plastered on his sweet face, took it all in stride and enjoyed bopping Dave on the head with his bandaged arm whenever he had the chance.

And the rest of that $2500 that had been raised? Two other young people's lives were also changed by such a small amount of money: a girl whose arm bone was severely infected left the hospital with her arm healthy and intact, and a young man who'd shattered both legs a year before was able to regain their use and return to a normal way of life. God had multiplied the faithful gifts of a few beyond the Bells' imagination.

Indeed the faithful gifts of American partners back home were always essential to Dave and Jen's ministry. Support, both spiritual and financial, from those back home is what keeps missionaries afloat and doing God's work. The Bells never took that for granted! How well they knew that the "senders" were every bit as crucial as those who had been sent, all working together for God's Kingdom. All their ministries were made possible by donations from those in the US who shared Dave and Jen's hearts to serve in Kenya.

One of those donors, an Indiana Rotary Club, provided funds to purchase and distribute the water purifier, PUR, developed by Proctor & Gamble, to villagers across Kenya. These are packets of chemicals when added to contaminated water, remove pathogenic microorganisms, purifying and making that water clean and safe to drink. A simple yet powerful ministry, this technology literally saved countless lives from diseases such as cholera, hepatitis, and severe diarrhea. The villagers often thought the packets were magical, transforming dirty brown water into crystal clear and drinkable water. Over time the Bells and their teams would distribute thousands and thousands of PUR packets across the country.

During their stint under HEART, Dave and Jen grew tremendously in experience and wisdom, learning many lessons that would benefit them in the years to come. But eventually, as is often said, all good things must come to an end and the Bells' time with HEART had reached that point. After some changes at HEART and some philosophical differences with the direction of that ministry, Dave and Jen had come to a fork in the road. Feeling once again that God was leading them in a different direction, in December 2007 they left HEART and their home in the HEART compound to join Christ's Hope International and moved to Kitengela.

Christ's Hope was not new to the Bells. In their eighteen months serving in Kenya, they had worked alongside CHI many times. God's timing always being perfect, at that particular time CHI was looking for someone to fill a gap in the administrative side of the ministry, writing policies for the multiple countries where the ministry was involved and helping to develop the "Choose to Wait" program. While administration had never been their chosen area of service or expertise, this was where God needed them to be for this season. When Dave and Jen parted ways with HEART, Christ's Hope was a great fit for the direction they felt God calling them at the time. But for the first time since moving to Africa, the Bells found themselves homeless and house-hunting.

God was way ahead of them. After a real estate agent had shown them several homes for rent in Kitengela, Dave and Jen were becoming frustrated. With a budget of 30-40,000 ksh per month (about $450-650 at the time), finding a home large enough for them as well as room to house visiting mission teams was looking to be a challenge. Sharing their desire to have more space, the agent mentioned a large house available but that it was outside of their budget. Immediately upon seeing the home, Dave and Jen knew this was where they wanted to be. The home was very nice by Kenyan standards, seven bedrooms on a small fenced compound with several fruit trees as well as a 16,000-gallon reserve water tank buried in the yard, a true luxury in Kenya. The asking rental price for the home was 70,000 ksh per month, twice what the Bells had intended to spend. As it turned out, the couple who owned the home were both doctors working in AIDS-related fields, and when they learned of the Bells' mission work were willing to lease it to them for 40,000 ksh. Yet another miraculous provision by God!

Transitions are challenging, and this one was particularly hard as Dave and Jen struggled through some emotional healing as well. Leaving HEART had been painful and somewhat unexpected, certainly not in their timing, leaving in its wake emotional casualties of human relationships and hurt feelings. God closed that door with a bang, and the Bells reeled from it for a while. Those few months were truly a dark time for them, a time of questioning whether they should even be in Kenya, a time of reevaluating their lives and wondering if maybe they had misunderstood God. They even considered packing their bags and heading back home. Yet they knew, deep down, that God was using even this painful lesson to refine them and lead them another direction.

And He had sent them Sarah. A good friend of the family from back in Indiana, Sarah Reese happened to be living in Kenya interning with Dave and Jen when this calamity hit. Sarah may have just been a teenager, but she brought Dave, Jen, and Nate much-needed laughter and sunshine to their dark clouds just when they needed it most. Sarah helped the Bells move and even did some minor interior decorating to make the Kitengela house feel like home. She was truly a God-send in this season of the Bells' lives.

By now Nate was a high school senior, finishing up his final weeks of schooling before traveling back to the US to continue his college education. That change was coming soon, and the anticipation of that change also hung in the air. Dave and Jen knew it would be difficult to let Nate fly, and yet that is exactly what they had reared him to do.

So many changes, with more on the horizon for the Bells. So much out of their control, yet they trusted that God was way ahead of them and would pave the way. If they would just continue to lick and turn…

CHAPTER 16

Hunkering Down

December 30, 2007

Kitengela, Kenya

Working at his desk in their new Kitengela home, Dave's cell phone dinged in his pocket. A text message from the US Embassy in Nairobi: High security alert, rioting and violence in Nairobi.

Dave let out a huge sigh as he read the text. Not the first security warning he'd received from the Embassy, nor would it be the last, but this one just felt different. This one made his pulse race a little faster. Somehow Dave knew this warning was serious.

Just three days earlier, on Thursday, December 27, 2007, the Kenyan people had flocked to the polls for their national elections, including the casting of ballots for their choice as President. This election had been hotly contested from the beginning, pitting current President Mwai Kibaki against challenger Raila Odinga. While tensions were often high as Election Day drew near, no one would have predicted what would transpire soon after.

Amidst undeniable evidence of vote-rigging and ballot manipulation ignored by Kenya's election commission in an apparent effort to keep the present government in power, that morning of December 30, Kibaki, of the Kikuyu tribe, had been declared the winner of the deeply controversial election. Supporters of Odinga, of the Luo tribe, were enraged at the obviously compromised result. Just fifteen minutes after Kibaki was declared the winner, a tribal war erupted.

Violent mayhem quickly spread through the city of Nairobi. Gangs of raging young Luo men burst into the streets, brandishing sticks, burning and smashing shacks, dragging Kikuyus out of their homes and beating them to death. The chaos quickly snowballed, eventually engaging thousands and thousands of people with Kenyan soldiers futilely attempting to restore order.

One of the hardest hit areas was the Mathare slums, where the daily norm of anarchy now turned into total pandemonium. Tribal loyalties ran deep in the Kenyan culture, and the unprotected slums, full of desperate, hopeless people with nothing much to lose, were raw, fertile staging grounds for violence.

Safe in their gated compound outside of Nairobi, the Bells hunkered down to ride out the storm, having no idea how long it would take for the situation to be defused. Dave's cell phone was their lifeline to the outside world, and the frequent reports of violence caused them to pray fervently for the safety of their friends in Nairobi and especially Mathare. The first night of rioting, Dave got a call from one of their connections in the slum. They had sheltered some children from the opposing tribe in their home, and as Dave talked he could hear the noise of the rioters trying to break through the door. That same night, Dave would learn, over 300 shack-homes in Mathare were burned down and hundreds killed. The sheltered children were safe, at least temporarily, but two young adults that Dave and Jen worked with had been beaten to death.

Another important conduit of information from the world outside their gates was the Bells' driver, Francis Macharia. Francis, the brother of Dave's handyman/gardener John Maina, was a part-time driver for Dave, helping transport visiting teams as needed. Francis lived just outside the slums and his keen ears picked up news from the slums and streets that he relayed to the Bells. Francis shared horrific stories of a whole different Kenya than the Bells had seen before...husbands killing wives who were of a different tribal background, buses being stopped and passengers forced to prove their tribal name by showing identification with those of the enemy tribe being killed on the spot. One sister of Francis and John was on such a bus and barely escaped with her life.

Sheltered in their safe haven, Dave, Jen, Nate, and their visiting friend Sarah did not feel immediate or life-threatening effects of the anarchy outside their gates, but the rioting certainly caused them much anxiety for their vulnerable friends, and it also didn't take long for them to feel the squeeze as supply lines were interrupted. Outside their gates, Kenyan society shut down for a time. No public transportation, no medications for hospitals and clinics, no shipments of food or commodities. Schools were closed indefinitely, and when they finally did open again, most were understaffed as many teachers had lost their lives in the violence.

While they had enough food inside the compound, after two weeks of hunkering down the Bells ventured out into the uncertain world beyond, a world with riot police stationed at every intersection, a world where even going into the Mathare slums with desperately-needed supplies was a very risky proposition. But the Bells went, nonetheless, and the carnage they saw on that initial trip after the riots was staggering. Large areas where ramshackle homes had once stood were smoldering and flattened, piles of tires still burning, angry crowds still shouting and protesting. Dead bodies were strewn everywhere, and they were horrified to discover the tiny form of a dead baby lying along the river, tossed onto the ground like an abandoned doll. But most heart-breaking of all were the children of Mathare, rushing into Dave, Jen, and Nate's arms, crying and sharing stories of terror. These precious little ones were living a nightmare in the most nightmarish of places, painting a catastrophic scene of death and destruction that would forever be seared into the Bells' minds.

Often Francis would get wind of an upcoming riot before it even happened, and he became a very valuable resource for Dave and Jen. In the weeks to come, Dave and Jen would count on Francis's knowledge and intuition to be sure it was safe for them to visit particular areas of Kenya. The rioting had been widespread and no one was immune to the danger, especially a white missionary family who might get caught in the crossfire of the tribal power struggle.

To add to their feelings of isolation, folks back home in the States were urging them to leave Kenya and come home. Having heard about the violence daily on the news, Dave's and Jen's families and friends were very concerned about their safety and didn't understand why they didn't just pull up stakes and move back to the US, at least for a time. Dave and Jen tried their best to allay their families' fears, minimizing the volatile situation as best they could in their communications home. But Dave and Jen insisted, even though many did not understand, that the safest place for them to be was in the center of their Father's will. As they sought God's direction during this new crisis, He made it clear to them that He still had much work for them to do right there in Kenya.

Over time, the violence slowly calmed down and by April 2008 a shaky truce had been negotiated. But the crisis was far from over. Hundreds of thousands of Kenyans had been left homeless, with women and children most affected. Refugee communities called IDP camps ("internally displaced persons") had been set up all over the country for those losing their homes in the violence. While official estimates put the number of riot deaths at around 1500, most believe the true number was probably much closer to 5000, with the lack of medicines to treat those who were HIV+ as well as dangerous living conditions and starvation taking hundreds more lives indirectly.

During these weeks, Dave and Jen often felt very helpless and useless. They could do nothing to stop the violence and rage, and they were very limited in what material help they were able to provide. Prayer was all they had, and daily they spent hours praying for relief for the thousands that were hurting. If Kenya had been a country of desperation before, now it was a nation in dire crisis, dark with physical need and even more dark spiritually. If ever a people needed Jesus....

Gradually, life began to get back to "normal" as slowly the Bells felt more and more comfortable going outside the compound to the countless needy people around them, made even more so by the rioting. Having just barely gotten their feet wet with Christ Hope International before the election disaster, they began to get their footing on how to proceed in this new direction. Part of their work with HEART had been doing youth abstinence programs with teenagers in schools and villages, teaching them about the sacredness of physical intimacy and the importance of reserving sexual relationships for marriage. Not only was this God's designed plan, but it also had tremendous ramifications to help stop the spread of the AIDS virus. Desiring to further expand this training, even before leaving HEART, Dave and Jen had been looking for an effective sexual purity curriculum with an international twist to use in this portion of their outreach.

They found it in Christ Hope International's "Choose to Wait" program, created by CHI founders who were from South Africa themselves and understood the African mindset. A solid Christian teaching on abstinence, Dave and Jen were excited about using this new tool in the schools and villages to which God led them. Along with that, they would be doing CHI's "Care and Compassion" program (education, nutrition, and medical care for those infected with HIV/AIDs), as well as seeking out OVCs (orphans and vulnerable children) to help.

They began laying groundwork for these new outreaches by meeting with local pastors, village chiefs, and school officials in the Kitengela area, as well as connecting with Compassion International to potentially partner with them in rural areas. Many schools in their immediate vicinity were open to and badly in need of the "Choose to Wait" teaching. Sexual promiscuity was the norm, every village had countless members infected by HIV or already suffering from AIDS, and OVCs were everywhere. The refugee camps, especially, were filled with terrified children trapped there who were raped and abused daily. One thing was certain, God was placing a plethora of ministry opportunities at the Bells' feet, and with each an open door to share the love and hope of Jesus with those hurting souls.

In March 2008, Dave and Jen traveled to Uganda to work with Compassion International setting up a "Choose to Wait" training for later in the year. While in Uganda they also met with the CHI board for that country, fulfilling part of their responsibilities as East Africa Representatives for CHI. In that role Dave and Jen would be traveling to all East Africa countries doing similar work.

God knew they would need their calendars full of ministry, as the Bells were quickly facing another milestone in their lives. At the end of March 2008, Nate finished his twelve years of schooling and boarded a plane back to the US...without his parents. Nate would live with his brother Chris and sister-in-law Ariel for a while while working and going to school, and for the first time in their lives Dave and Jen became "empty-nesters." As exciting as it was, the transition was also difficult for all of them. Doing ministry overseas side-by-side for so many years had built a special bond between Nate and his parents, and adjusting to their new lives was hard for all of them. Keeping busy was the perfect antidote to the sadness Dave and Jen felt as they put their youngest on the airplane to fly home.

As with most missionary couples, the Bells always built a furlough into their calendar, a time to go home to see family as well as connect with donors in the States. The six- to eight-week furlough was always much-anticipated, but by the end of that time, while it was certainly hard to leave family behind yet again, Dave and Jen were always ready to go back "home" to Kenya. "Home," they had learned over the years, was an ambiguous term. Jen often defined "home" as where she laid her head at night. But they both knew and held onto the promise that their real "home" wasn't here on earth at all, that they were just sojourners here and their true Home was in Heaven with their Father.

Following their summer furlough that year, the new empty-nesters hit the ground running pretty much as soon as their airplane wheels touched down on the Nairobi runway. Their schedule for the remainder of 2008 filled quickly. Countless visits were made to hospitals and homes visiting AIDs victims, helping provide the medicines and assistance they needed to carry on as best they could. Sometimes that meant bringing the disease into a manageable state so a father could return to a life where he could provide for his family. Oftentimes that meant praying and sharing God's love with one of His children very close to death. It was heart-wrenching and frustrating, yet Dave and Jen continued to be inspired by the strength and hope many of these people still had in the midst of desperate circumstances, hanging onto Jesus in the face of death.

Not only were the Bells' neck-deep in hands-on ministry, they were also trying to learn the administrative ropes of Christ Hope International - Kenya. They had agreed to serve as CHI's Kenya Mission and Volunteer Coordinators, as well as taking on the roles of CHI's East Africa Representatives. Jen's gifts of organization served them well as they worked with the CHI Kenya Managing Committee to put into place many new policies, documents, and procedures geared toward strengthening and deepening the effects of the ministry as well as improving accountability and integrity with the donors and partners. Each tiny step of change was a struggle and oftentimes led to frustration, but slowly Dave and Jen became integrated into the inner workings of CHI – Kenya.

Marriage, even under the easiest of circumstances, is challenging. Add to the normal stresses of marriage the extra tensions of living in a foreign country with no real family support, financial concerns, constant exhaustion, feelings of hopelessness and uselessness, and serving side-by-side 24/7, and it's easy to see how many missionary couples' marriages end in divorce. Even the strongest Christian values are hard to maintain in such a divisive atmosphere, and Satan surely uses those weak cracks in relationships to attack.

Even though Dave and Jen had always enjoyed a strong loving relationship, they were not exempt from some difficult times in their marriage. Suffering through the hurtful separation from their HEART family and the subsequent move, sending their son off to his own adult life leaving just the two of them for the first time, and often being overwhelmed adjusting to CHI and bombarded with ill and needy Kenyans at every turn, the Bells found themselves too often taking their weariness and frustrations out on each other. In God's timing, just when the couple needed it most He provided an opportunity for them to work through the "Love Dare" book, based on the movie "Fireproof," together. It literally changed their lives! After 26 years of marriage, both Dave and Jen found they still had much to learn about how best to complete each other and they grew both individually and together. The study sparked deeper communication and better understanding about how God had wired each of them, and truly reinforced their commitment to each other in ways they never dreamed possible. God knew exactly what this struggling couple needed to bolster them to continue serving Him.

Steadily Dave and Jen settled into life in Kitengela, serving the Lord in this spot on the globe where He'd led. Despite the difficulties, the danger, and the frustrations that life in Kenya brought, the Bells hunkered down and settled in for the ministry work He placed before them.

CHAPTER 17

Refining and Defining

July 2009

Kitengela, Kenya

Jen snuggled the tiny swaddled infant in her arms, softly singing to him as her hand gently stroked his tight black curls. Smiling with contentment even though it was the middle of the night following a very long, busy day, Jen's mind flashed back to her childhood when she'd cuddled a runty piglet much like she was nestling this weensie human. His black skin created a stark contrast next to her white arm, an insignificant detail that carried no importance in neither her nor God's eyes. A beautiful, albeit tiny, child of God was in her tender care for now and Jen was savoring every moment.

Baby David had been born prematurely just a couple of days earlier, abandoned to die in the slums of Nairobi with his umbilical cord still attached and pebbles pushed into his nose and ears. Weighing less than 4 pounds, survival of this tiny boy seemed unlikely. But saving unlikely lives was Jen's specialty, and when they received the call asking if the Bells might be willing to care for him until other arrangements could be made, Dave and Jen didn't think twice. Quickly scraping together some basic supplies and purchasing formula, they brought the baby into their home, bathed and fed him, and showered him the most important human need of all, lots of touch and love.

Within a few days, David was already showing signs of thriving and the Bells reluctantly but necessarily took him to a local children's home, Brydges Centre, where Dave and Jen had made many visits since moving into the area. No sooner had they said good-bye to Baby David when Dave's phone rang again and they were off once more to bring another baby into their home, this time a little boy who had been given up for adoption by his single mother who couldn't feed the five other children she already had.

Slowly but surely, God had been refining their ministry since the Bells had moved to Kitengela seven months ago. As they'd worked in all three areas of CHI-Kenya's outreach, the Orphans and Vulnerable Children program had become the one dearest to their hearts. True, they had enjoyed training and teaching teens the "Choose to Wait" program and had also touched many, many lives of AIDS/HIV victims to whom they'd ministered through the "Care and Compassion" outreaches in hospitals and villages. Kenya was filled with desperate people of all ages with many different needs, and Dave and Jen were humbled to be Jesus's hands and feet in many situations.

But the children. Oh, the children. Helping the children, the most innocent victims of all, that was Dave and Jen's real passion. It took a while for them to realize it, but God had been refining their ministry these past years, subtly chipping away other areas of ministry to allow them time and energy to focus more and more on the children. When the Bells discovered the under-staffed children's homes were often ill-equipped to handle the demands of caring for abandoned newborns, they offered their assistance to shoulder some of the load until the babies were of a more manageable age. The children's homes were overjoyed with the offer, and Baby David began a steady trickle of newborns into and out of the Bells' temporary care. Some babies stayed just a few days, others a couple of weeks depending on the need and Dave and Jen's availability.

As their hearts turned more and more toward the nurturing of these rescued babies, gradually they backed away from other ministries. It was a slow progression that Dave and Jen didn't even realize was happening at the time, but as babies came into their lives they had less time to devote in other directions. Even when they weren't caring for infants in their home, it seemed that special children kept crossing their path. Children they would never forget.

Like Nickel. Dave first noticed Nickel following him around the local convenience store in the small town of Athi River, dressed in filthy rags but always with a big grin on his dirty face. Nickel was obviously mentally handicapped and later Dave would find out he was also epileptic. While many would have found Nickel to be a nuisance and shooed him away, these store employees had sort of adopted this little ragamuffin ten-year-old who lived just across the street, sharing a small ramshackle shelter right next to the open sewer with his family of eight. The store workers patiently allowed Nickel to push around a child's shopping cart and put things in it then take them back out, pretending he was buying things. Nickel spoke only in grunts and laughter, and Dave grew fond of him and looked forward to Nickel rushing across the street when he saw Dave enter the store. Nickel "helped" Dave with his shopping and Dave would reward him with a treat of yogurt or juice.

One day some months later when Dave entered the store, the manager came to Dave with Nickel in tow. For the first time ever, Nickel was not smiling or laughing. Apparently during an epileptic seizure several days before, Nickel had fallen into a fire and severely burned his hand and arm. No one had taken him for medical treatment, instead smearing Vaseline on it and wrapping it up. By the time Dave saw it, the hand was badly infected and two of the fingers were black from gangrene.

Dave had a mission team with him at the time, so he phoned John to take Nickel to the local clinic and Dave met them there as soon as he was able. Walking through the clinic door an hour later, Dave was rushed by Nickel who grabbed him and wouldn't let go. Never having seen a doctor before and obviously in great pain, Nickel was terrified.

Nickel's injuries were much too serious for the clinic to handle, and the next day Dave, Jen, and John went to Athi River to drive Nickel and his aunt to the Kijabe Hospital. Now eleven years old and never having left Athi River, Nickel was in awe the entire drive. The large cement factories, tall buildings, and whizzing traffic of Nairobi amazed him. Outside the city Nickel saw zebras and giraffes grazing in the seemingly endless fields, and further on, as the vehicle descended into the Great Rift Valley, Nickel's eyes opened wide as he gazed across miles and miles of green valley shadowed by towering mountains. The child had seen a world that he never even imagined existed.

Although the hospital experience frightened Nickel, miraculously doctors were able to save much more of his hand than initially thought. Despite the widespread infection, the only amputation that was needed was one joint of the index finger. Eventually Nickel's hand healed well enabling him to lead a normal life. Understandably, Nickel earned a special place in Dave and Jen's heart.

Then there was Edwin, a ten-year-old living at the Brydges Children's Center when Dave and Jen met him in 2004 on their first Kenya trip. Edwin had told them that day that he was going to be a pilot, and each time Dave and Jen saw this little boy he reiterated his dream of flying airplanes. Edwin's eyes would light up when the Bells would bring him books about aviation to encourage him, but deep down they knew it was an extremely long shot that this orphan would ever be able to realize his dream. Not only was the pilot school very elite and selective with only the "cream of the crop" ever having a chance of being admitted, the cost to attend was prohibitive. It seemed impossible that even if Edwin could make the necessary grades he'd ever be able to afford to attend such an exclusive school when even simple needs like food were difficult to supply.

But nothing is impossible with God. Over the years Edwin never wavered in his dedication to his dream, working diligently to earn top grades and eventually being chosen out of twenty of his peers to attend the elite school. While elated at this opportunity, by now

Edwin was well aware of the financial reality, and he prayed and fasted for an entire week as he sought God's provision to realize his dream. When Dave and Jen shared the news that some special friends in the States had provided the funds for Edwin to go to school, he didn't need a pilot's license as he was already soaring above the clouds with joy!

Edwin would go on not only to excel in pilot's school, but to be one of its very top students. Even more importantly, Edwin was sharing the gospel with fellow students by leading a Bible study for over 150 fellow students, as well as being outspoken about God's plan for sexual abstinence before marriage. Edwin would go on to become a commercial pilot for Kenya Airways, a very prestigious job for any Kenyan and a seemingly impossible dream-come-true for a penniless orphan boy. Edwin would forever inspire Dave and Jen, humbling them with his living example of faith and perseverance.

By the end of 2009, another transition was in the works. As God was refining the Bells' ministry and pointing them more and more toward orphans and vulnerable children, He also was opening another door of opportunity. With the two-year commitment to serving under Christ Hope International coming near its end, Dave and Jen were ready for a change. They'd made great progress on the administrative side for CHI, gaining valuable experience that God knew they would need later, but those days spent traveling to Namibia and Germany for meetings and hours spent formulating policies on the computer was lost time they weren't able to spend doing the ministry on which they thrived. Hands-on, face-to-face, intimate interactions were what the Bells loved most, and both Dave and Jen were anxious to get back to using those gifts and sharing the gospel on a personal basis.

And so, beginning in January 2010, the Bells left their positions at Christ Hope International to begin serving under a new organization headquartered in Muncie, Indiana, just a few miles from their childhood stomping grounds, Christian Service International Ministries. As Dave and Jen transitioned into the CSI organization, they also transitioned back into the heart of their missionary passion…being the practical hands and feet of Jesus to God's children.

Much time was spent working with the children and management of the Brydges Center, home to about eighty children. Dave and Jen had become quite involved over the past couple of years, regularly taking visiting teams to the home and helping out wherever needed, as well as doing teaching sessions to encourage the staff. Taking in more and more orphans, the home was bursting at the seams and had children spread throughout several rental properties in order to accommodate them all. Sorely in need of more living space, the management had ambitiously begun plans to build a new home and the Bells jumped onboard to help. Building anything in Kenya was a huge and often frustrating undertaking, especially for task-oriented, time-conscious Americans. Besides the obvious challenge of raising money, there were plenty of other challenges -- obtaining water permits and building permits, securing reliable building contractors, dealing with fluctuating material prices, and finding trustworthy workers being just a few. What a joyous cause for celebration when on March 7, 2010, Dave was privileged to give the morning worship message at the new Brydges Center ground-breaking!

God knew that Dave and Jen would need to learn all these lessons and more for the future plans He had in store for them, but of which they did not yet have an inkling. And so, side by side with the Brydges staff, the Bells and their teams worked to build the new Brydges Center. Much of their first year with CSI, 2010, was spent on this massive project. Teams assisted wherever they could, not only with the construction itself but also by landscaping with one team planting several hundred bougainvilleas along the new property fence line. Another team purchased and assembled a 26'x40' greenhouse as well as planting a half-acre shamba (garden) which would provide fresh vegetables and fruits for the children in the home. And all of these projects, of course, provided plenty of opportunities to love on and minister to the children living there who were starving for human interaction.

Another new project initiated during those first few months with CSI was The Kujitegemea Project. The Swahili word "kujitegemea" means "self-sufficient," and that was exactly what the goal of this project was: empowering Kenyan families to provide for themselves. As has been proven over and over again in developing countries, just handing out funds is not a long-term solution to helping people escape poverty. This project would provide small business loans to individuals to whom banks would not lend money due to their poverty and health, loans that would enable them to start new businesses or enlarge existing ones, businesses such as operating a small booth to sell bananas or avocados. As the new business made money, the owners would repay the loan which would provide funds for yet another family to begin a business. Not only would the business have a long-term positive financial impact, but it would also help build self-esteem and confidence as families would be able to provide for themselves.

An essential component to making The Kujitegemea Project a success was weekly sessions with potential new business owners, teaching them basic skills in finance, how to write a business plan, money management, and perhaps most importantly, basic truths from God's Word on how to handle money and possessions. Their financial training years before through Larry Burkett's Christian Financial Concepts classes had developed a passion within Dave and Jen to help others learn how to handle their money wisely and in line with Biblical teaching. Once more God had been training them for their ministry in Kenya long before they dreamed of becoming missionaries!

Starting up this program was a huge undertaking, as the Bells knew that for it to succeed well the Kenyans needed to ultimately have ownership in it. After working with Kenyans to organize it and do the initial training, the plan was for the Bells to gradually back out and work behind the scenes. Dave and Jen spent much time praying for wisdom and discernment on how best to maintain this sensitive balance.

Water projects were also a major focus of the Bells during this time, often working alongside long-time friends Mark and Camille Purington and helping with their Eleos Project ministry. Not only did they continue distributing the PUR water packets as often as they were able, they had an opportunity to begin working in rural Maasai villages to help them obtain clean water. The Maasai culture values livestock, especially cattle, more than human life and the village and herds use the same water sources. The Bells, with the help of donor churches and groups in the US, began replacing parts to repair existing hand pumps that had been damaged by elephants and left abandoned and also assisted in the financing and drilling of new boreholes. While the AIDS/HIV epidemic was devastating Maasai villages as well as other Kenyan populations, water-borne diseases took their own toll, with three out of every five infant deaths under the age of five attributed to illnesses caused by contaminated water.

How fitting that water became part of the Bells' ministry, as it also gave them the perfect illustration to teach about the Living Water that only Jesus gives to a hard-to-reach people such as the Maasai. As Jesus said in John 4: 13-14: *"Everyone who drinks of this water will be thirsty again, but whoever drinks of the water that I will give him will never be thirsty again. The water that I will give him will become in him a spring of water welling up to eternal life."*

Working on water projects in the Maasai villages gave Dave and Jen access to other whole groups of malnourished and unhealthy children. Introducing them to peanut butter sandwiches, the Bells were able to get some much-needed protein into their diets. Peanut butter was a food that the Maasai had never eaten, but just the introduction of this one food caused a noticeable improvement in some weak Maasai children. In addition to peanut butter, the Bells also provided food staples of beans and rice to village families, and along with the physical nutrition came the opportunities to share the spiritual food that they so desperately needed even more.

These, however, were not the safest of times to be Americans in Kenya. Daily fresh threats from surrounding terrorist nations targeting Americans reached their ears. Dave and Jen were ever more cautious about where they were going and kept abreast on what was happening around them. Car-jackings increased and there were constant rumblings of possible terrorist attacks brewing against Westerners in Kenya. While they were extra-diligent to the volatile climate, thankfully the Bells were never directly in harm's way and they continually prayed for God's protection over them while they continued about His work.

In September 2010 God led a wonderful nurse to cross Dave and Jen's path, a medical professional who had worked as a missionary in Kenya with World Gospel Mission's "The Least of These" ministry for many years already and who would become a dear friend and ministry partner for the Bells. Robyn Moore was even a fellow Hoosier, giving them another bond of familiarity, and her contagious smile and understanding of the challenges of missionary work in this country offered much-needed encouragement over the years. Dave and Jen first met Robyn at a medical clinic she was conducting at a children's home, and Jen, herself a medical professional, was a wonderful help as Robyn examined and treated the children. That friendship forged in late 2010 would become a huge asset for the Bells as God continued to lead them where He intended.

Without warning, the lives of the Bells were about to pivot again. Unbeknownst to Dave and Jen at the time, they were about to fall in love. And God would use that love to bring them to the ministry for which He'd been laying the foundation all these years. All the puzzle pieces were beginning to fall into place...

CHAPTER 18

Michael Moses

December 2010

Kitengela, Kenya

Perhaps it was his enormous brown eyes that seemed to connect his soul to their heart. Perhaps it was his condition, one of the weakest and most pitiful infants upon whom Dave and Jen had ever laid their eyes. Perhaps it was the way his tiny brown fingers wrapped around their own white ones with a strength belied by his tiny frame, as if holding on to his only chance for survival. Perhaps it was his spirit, a child who by all accounts should have perished yet was still fiercely clinging to life.

Whatever it was, Michael Moses stole Dave and Jen's hearts the moment they first saw him in December 4, 2010. Little did they know it that day, but their lives would never be the same.

Michael's origin was unremarkable, an unwanted newborn born in February 2010, abandoned and left to die on the streets of the Mathare slums, a tragic scenario by now all too familiar to the Bells and Nurse Robyn. Rescued by a community health worker, Michael had been taken to a nearby children's home for care. When Robyn first saw him in April, she approximated his age at about six weeks old and he weighed 3 kg (6.5 pounds), seemingly normal, although a bit small for his age.

As Robyn periodically did clinic checks on Michael, she became quite concerned about his welfare. Not only did he often have unexplained rodent bites and lesions, he was also ill with respiratory problems and ear infections and needed a couple of hospitalizations. Even more worrisome, Michael was not gaining weight, failing to thrive and continually getting weaker. By the time Dave and Jen first met Michael, at ten months old he was unable to sit or stand, had difficulty swallowing, and was drastically malnourished as he weighed less than 5 kg (under 11 pounds).

Jen could not take her eyes off this precious pitiful child. Jen knew that if Michael were left in the home he would soon die there, and she believed with all her heart that if she could just take Michael home with her, she would be able to improve his health status through proper nutrition, therapy, and plenty of loving care. At the urging of Robyn, the director of the home finally agreed to release Michael into the Bells' care, giving them temporary custody for a short time.

Her heart fluttering with nervous excitement, Jen carried little Michael to their van and placed him in the car seat. This was her passion, this was what she was born to do, to care for those most vulnerable and helpless, giving them a chance at life. God had placed this very sick little child, who could barely hold up his head, into her nurturing arms!

Michael's turn-around was nearly immediate and remarkable. He began eating and gaining weight, quickly becoming stronger and mobile and catching up on developmental milestones. He began smiling and laughing, and by May of 2011 Michael was crawling, standing, and cruising. In the months that Dave and Jen had Michael, they also discovered that the home where he'd been living did not have proper legal status and therefore had no legal rights to give temporary custody to the Bells. The only way to keep Michael, it seemed, was to open a registered children's home themselves. And so, after much prayer and seriously considering all it entailed, they began to take the legal actions necessary to register as a children's home.

When the children's home director saw the dramatic improvement in Michael's health, she began insisting that he be returned to the care of the center. The Bells and Robyn resisted, knowing full well that Michael had not received proper care when previously at the home and they feared his return would halt his progress. Dave and Jen petitioned the court to become Michael's foster parents, which was vehemently fought by the home's director. Because they were not yet registered with the government as a legal children's home, the Bells were not granted permission to foster the baby. With Michael's well-being and safety being the top priority in a contentious and possibly even dangerous situation, in July 2011 they were ordered to place Michael in a different children's home three hours away.

Dave and Jen were in tears as they left the crying child with his new caretakers. They had come to love Michael as their own child, spending countless hours nurturing him and showering him with love. Although they didn't know his exact day of birth, in February they had celebrated his first birthday with a party and cake. Deep in their hearts, they had known all too well that Michael's tenure with them might be temporary but they hoped perhaps God would open the door for them to permanently become his

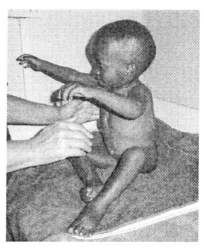

Michael Moses   August 2011

legal guardians or perhaps even adopt him. That might have been their plan, but it was not God's plan.

But God had used Michael Moses in a powerful way that would impact the lives of many babies for years to come. Just before Michael's departure, the Bells' petition to become a registered children's home was approved, although because they had previously cared for Michael they were not legally allowed to adopt him. Even though he would never be their adopted child, this small child had a profound influence which forever changed the direction of the Bells' ministry.

Michael Moses may have been just a toddler, but he and God were leading the Bells down a new ministry path, causing them to lick and turn once again.

CHAPTER 19

Mahali pa Maisha

August 2011

Kitengela, Kenya

A Place of Life.

Their new infant rescue center was certainly living up to its name. The Bells' home was filled with sounds of life, baby life...squeals, giggles, cries, jabbering, a beautiful cacophony of sound coming from the four infants now under Dave and Jen's care.

Three months earlier, in May 2011, under the jurisdiction of the Children's Department of Kajiado North District, Dave and Jen, still working under Christian Service International, had become founders of this brand new infant rescue center they aptly named Mahali pa Maisha. "Mahali pa Maisha" is Swahili for the phrase "a place of life," and that was just what Dave and Jen envisioned as they embarked on this new path to which God through Michael Moses had led them. After prayerful consideration, the Bells decided that the stated purpose and mission statement of this new ministry would be: "Mahali pa Maisha, Swahili for 'A Place of Life,' shows the love of Jesus Christ and shares His hope by enriching the overall holistic health of abandoned babies and vulnerable children."

Starting MpM was not a decision the Bells took lightly. It was a huge commitment and they knew it. But lately they had been challenged by their personal Bible study, challenged to be bold and step out in faith. Weeks of intense prayer, fact-finding sessions with others, and many long discussions between themselves preceded the day they turned in the paperwork. God had placed an undeniable burden on their hearts for the most needy, innocent, and voiceless of all. Babies.

Michael's situation had finally brought their passion to the forefront. Over the years Dave and Jen had seen many "Michaels," children who were caught in the tangled legal web of the Kenyan system. Not only were they not being cared for properly, as most Kenyan children's homes were overcrowded and understaffed, but getting these children into loving families was an uphill battle. Adoption was frowned upon in Kenyan culture, and making a child even available for adoption required a tedious yet essential paper trail that most children's homes did not have the manpower or energy to pursue. So many children were growing up, if they lived that long, in children's homes with no family roots, which are a vital part of Kenyan culture. Spending their early developmental years in an institutional setting instead of the God-designed family was an additional emotional challenge for children already dealing with so much heartache.

And while there were many children's homes in Kenya, there were very few that were properly equipped to care for infants. Abandoned babies were a huge problem and most children's homes simply did not have the staff and resources to meet the demands of an infant, especially a high-risk one. Mahali pa Maisha would help fill that gap, providing holistic care to these most vulnerable of God's children with the goal of helping them get adopted into their own forever families.

If Dave and Jen had any lingering doubts about whether God wanted them to open an infant rescue center in that area of Kenya, they were dashed one day while helping with a medical clinic at one of the children's homes. A newborn infant was carried out, just a few days old and in very poor physical shape. When Dave saw this pitiful little girl, he asked the director why they would even take in an infant in this condition knowing that they did not have the resources to keep her alive. The director's reply was heart-wrenching. "If this one dies we can always get another one." Dave and Jen left that home even more determined to start Mahali pa Maisha as soon as possible.

Although it took several months before MpM became legally registered with the government of Kenya, the home began operating very much as it had before the Bells decided to make it official. Dave and Jen assisted the overcrowded and understaffed children's homes by taking in high-risk and care-demanding newborns and babies for short-term care, giving them the individual attention they needed to get them strong and healthy and back on track developmentally, only to have to take them back to a home that was not able to provide the proper care to maintain their health. But until MpM received its registration and was allowed to admit babies, it was the best help they could provide.

Even while Michael Moses was still living with them, the calls began coming. Word was getting out, and the district children's officer with whom the Bells had worked as they unsuccessfully tried to gain legal custody of Michael was already referring special needs babies to Mahali pa Maisha.

A Place of Life. It was a fitting name for this daunting ministry. When Dave had asked his artist friend back in the States to design a logo for MpM, he insisted that starfish be incorporated into the drawing. One life at a time. That had

always been their mantra. In a seashore of need, one little human starfish life at a time.

Over the course of their years in Kenya, God had masterfully been orchestrating this very ministry. It was no coincident that the Bells had made the connections and friendships that they had formed. It was no coincident that, even though administration was not their cup of tea, God had provided that season under Christ Hope International for Dave and Jen to learn the Kenyan-law ropes and how to develop policies and procedures and form a trust. It was no coincident that they had just so happened to find a large, multi-bedroom home for a modest price when only the two of them would eventually be living there. It was no coincident that Michael Moses had come into their world and caused them to fight, for him and the thousands of others like him. In God's world, there are no such things as coincidences. Only God-incidences!

And so, in God's infinite wisdom and marvelous provision, every single lesson, every experience, every success and failure, every realized dream and shattered hope throughout the Bells' lives had led up to this pivotal moment. They had been called out of their comfortable American-dream lives eleven years ago for this very ministry, Mahali pa Maisha, a place of life.

With the formation of Mahali pa Maisha came added financial responsibility. Dave and Jen immediately felt the pressure to raise more funds to ensure they could adequately provide for the children committed to their care. They began fundraising more earnestly than ever before, challenging friends and donors to join them in rescuing babies. As more and more infants came under their care, more and more money was needed to buy formula and supplies for them. Thankfully their home was plenty big, for the time being at least, to house several infants comfortably.

Michael also awakened an unexpected desire deep within the Bells that brought them to their knees seeking God's wisdom and direction. Having fallen in love with this special child, Dave and Jen thought the best and perhaps only way to protect Michael would be to adopt him. And so, after much prayer and many thoughtful discussions, the Bells set the wheels in motion to try to adopt this little boy. It was not a decision to be taken lightly -- adopting a child would be a lifetime commitment. Many hours were spent talking it through and praying for God's will and leading. When both Dave and Jen were sure that God was calling them to adopt, they turned in the application and turned the situation over to God.

It was not to be. Soon after Dave and Jen filled out the adoption papers, they found out that Kenyan adoption laws generally do not allow caretakers to adopt a child that had been under their temporary care. Dave and Jen were not eligible to become Michael's forever parents.

Despite the tremendous disappointment that they could likely never adopt Michael, the adoption process itself had already been set into motion. Both Dave and Jen still felt a strong desire to adopt a Kenyan child. While they still had slim hopes that perhaps that child might be Michael, even if he wasn't the child God had chosen for them, the Bells both felt they had been called to adopt. Kenyan culture discourages adoption, and the Bells had been constantly trying to change that mindset and convince Kenyans that adoption is a wonderful way to build a family. So in part, Dave and Jen thought if they adopted a Kenyan child they could be a practical example to those around them. But it was much more than that, the desire to adopt ran much deeper than just to serve as role models. Their hearts craved another child. Even though their two sons were grown and they would be older parents, the Bells felt that God had not yet completed their family.

It was during this period of waiting and wondering that God brought Christian into their lives. Conducting a medical clinic at a nearby children's home, Nurse Robyn was alarmed at the deteriorating condition of the fourteen-month-old little boy she examined and asked the Bells to take Christian under their care in hopes his health would improve. Lethargic with the distended belly of malnourishment,

Christian was weak and very sick and struggled to eat. Jen patiently worked with Christian, eventually getting him to keep foods down and yet he still wasn't gaining. After two weeks with little noticeable progress, Jen wondered about the possibility of food allergies and soon discovered that even though he would eat them, Christian was allergic to dairy products as well as bananas.

Six weeks after he came under the Bells' care, Christian was a changed child. Not only was he eating well and gaining weight, his belly was no longer swollen and his legs and arms had become strong. He was standing, walking with assistance, talking, laughing, and full of energy. It was an incredible turn-around, and when Christian returned to the children's home at the end of July 2010, he was truly a living example of God's miraculous power.

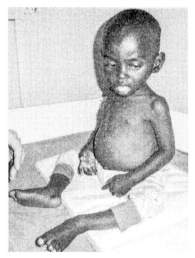
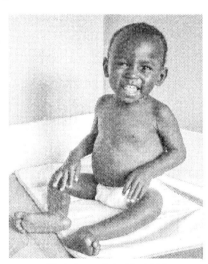

Christian   June 13, 2010   *Christian   July 27, 2010*

As Dave and Jen cared for Christian and other babies entrusted for brief stints to their care, they waited for the child God had chosen for them. And while they waited, Baby Talitha entered their lives and broke their hearts a little more.

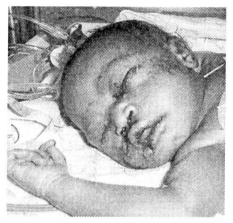
Talitha   August 13, 2011

On the morning of Friday, August 12, 2011, Dave's phone rang…a call from the District Children's Officer about an abandoned newborn she wanted them to take in. At her instruction, they arrived at the local police station to hear the story and receive the necessary papers allowing them to take the little girl home, and headed to the hospital where she had been admitted.

What they saw at the hospital sent shivers down their spine and brought tears to their eyes. This precious little girl, who Jen named Talitha ("little girl" in Aramaic) after the little girl written about in the Gospel of Mark that Jesus raised from the dead, had been born in the very early morning hours and dropped into a pit latrine. Someone going in hours later to use the choo had heard the newborn's weak whimpers about 6:30 a.m. and by-standers dismantled the structure and managed to rescue the newborn from the outdoor toilet pit. Not only was Talitha suffering with abrasions from the drop of several feet, her little body was covered with maggots that had already begun to consume her.

The hospital staff had been cleaning Talitha since her arrival, flushing every bodily orifice and suctioning out her nostrils and stomach frequently. When the Bells arrived, a tragic sight greeted them. Tiny Talitha was lying in an incubator, wrapped in cotton and covered in sores, with maggots continually crawling out of every opening in her body even hours after her arrival. All Dave and Jen could do was reach through the incubator hand holes and stroke her tiny tortured body, loving on her, singing softly, and praying for her. Doctors told Dave and Jen that Talitha not only had abrasions all over her body but also some "small cuts" on her private areas. She was given antibiotics and initially the doctors thought she was doing remarkably well considering her dire condition and hoped to be able to release her to the Bells' care in a couple of days.

When the hospital's senior medical officer saw her, he immediately insisted she be taken to another hospital as he feared they could not handle potential complications with her case. So Dave and Jen decided to take her to the Karen Hospital in Nairobi, which had just opened and was the most advanced hospital in the vicinity, knowing they would be best-equipped to handle an infant in her condition. Dave hung her IV bag from the safari roof of his truck and Jen held her close as they made the 90-minute drive to Karen. As Jen carried her in and the two of them stood by and watched, the hospital staff immediately began working on Talitha. They put her in front of a heater which was too hot, unintentionally blistering her skin. Jen noticed it and quickly moved the heater away, but not before her tender newborn skin had already started peeling from the burn. But that wasn't the worst of it. As the nurses washed her, it became very obvious that her condition was much more serious than anyone thought.

Those "minor cuts" in Talitha's female parts turned out to be major trauma unlike anything the hospital had ever seen. Whether it was caused by her birth, from being dropped, or something deliberately done to her would never be known. What they did know was that Talitha was in critical condition and in need of major medical assistance.

As Talitha fought for her life, Dave and Jen sent out urgent pleas to prayer warriors across the globe to pray for this precious little girl as well as her unidentified yet obviously desperate mother, a young woman who was seen leaving the latrine acting suspiciously then running away into the dark streets.

All day Saturday, Dave and Jen spent beside her ICU incubator, and when they left the hospital emotionally exhausted that evening they felt a peace that God would take care of Talitha.

And He did. Sunday morning as they sat in church, Dave got a call. God had done just what they asked. He had taken care of Talitha and welcomed her into His arms.

Dave and Jen were at a loss. Dealing with the death of an infant was something they had thankfully never experienced. The hospital suggested they bury her at Langata Cemetery where the homeless and destitute were buried. That was not an option for Talitha. After talking with the director of a children's home they had worked with many times, a person they trusted and knew had sadly dealt with situations like this before, she guided them through the legal aspects and invited them to lay Talitha to rest in their private cemetery at the home.

Sunday afternoon, Dave and Jen found themselves driving once more into the slums of Mathare, this time in search of an infant coffin in the only place they knew they could find one. They went back to Karen Hospital to pick up Talitha's tiny body from the morgue and Dave secluded himself in the garage painting the casket and preparing her little body for her funeral the following morning.

Talitha's Funeral   August 15, 2011

Talitha's funeral was brief yet a beautiful tribute to a precious child of God whose journey on this earth was tragically short and unbelievably painful. Yet in her three-day lifetime, Talitha impacted more hearts across the globe than most people will touch in decades. Dave gave the message and many of the home's staff members attended to say their earthly farewell to this little soul.

Dealing with hard stuff was a daily occurrence for the Bells since they had come to live in Kenya, but the experience with Talitha had a profound effect on them. Their hearts shattered, they couldn't help but question God. Why would He allow an innocent child to be born only to suffer like that? What had been Talitha's purpose? Yet despite all their questioning, they never doubted God's sovereignty, and despite the fact they didn't understand, they trusted that Talitha's life purpose had been fulfilled and took great comfort in the knowledge that this precious little girl was now whole and complete at home in the arms of Jesus.

A couple of purposes for Talitha's brief earthly sojourn were immediately apparent. The horrific circumstances surrounding her birth and life restoked the Bells' fire of passion for the most innocent victims in Kenya and reiterated their vision for founding Mahali pa Maisha. They were to be a voice for the voiceless, hope for the hopeless, a refuge for the abandoned, life for the unwanted, and Dave and Jen took that mission relentlessly to heart. Talitha's plight also connected to many supporters back in the States, putting a real-life story to the ministry the Bells were doing. Hundreds of people were praying for this little girl and through that experience many became partners both financially and spiritually with the MpM ministry.

On Christmas weekend 2011, the Bells were overjoyed to receive word that their registration for Mahali pa Maisha to be a Charitable Children's Institution had been approved by the Kenyan government. They were official! Now Dave and Jen could legally care for infants and facilitate adoptions for little ones in their care. Shortly after that, the CSI Kenya Trust they had applied for was also granted, meaning they were now fully registered and incorporated so they could legally own land in Kenya. After many long waits, much frustrating paperwork, and jumping through countless legal hoops, MpM was finally legal.

As if that wasn't excitement enough, the Bells began 2012 with a trip in early January to bring home their third son. What a shock to discover that the child God had chosen for them at the children's home was the very same precious now-22-month-old Christian who Dave and Jen had cared for six months previously! The adoption agency had no idea that the Bells knew Christian before, and even when Dave and Jen reluctantly disclosed that fact it didn't seem to matter. Since their oldest son was named Christopher, Dave and Jen decided to change Christian's name, and Ethan Levi Bell became their soon-to-be adopted son. Just four months later, in May 2012, beautiful nine-month-old Selah Grace Bell completed the Bell family. After the requisite three-month foster period, both adoptions were finalized. God had blessed them beyond all expectations!

As soon as Mahali pa Maisha became legal, the floodgates of infants opened up and babies needing special care began arriving. Abigail Susan was their first official admittance, coming to them the end of January 2012. Others quickly followed, each baby with his/her own unique story. Oftentimes infants came to them through other children's homes, sometimes through the District Children's Officer, and other times through a direct phone call from the police station. Never did they turn a baby away that was within their means to help. They were registered to care for newborn infants through toddlers up to two years old, and their once large, empty house quickly filled with cribs, infant supplies, and noisy babies.

It didn't take long for Dave and Jen to realize that they couldn't do this ministry alone, so gradually they added staff and trained them to help Jen care for the babies. Requirements for employment were strict and applications scrutinized, so only the most qualified and capable Christian women were chosen as MpM staff. Expectations and standards were high, but the staff was treated well and paid generously and a position working at Mahali pa Maisha was a wonderful opportunity for these young women.

The infant rescue center was the focal point of the Mahali pa Maisha ministry, but other spokes of ministry radiated from that hub. Building greenhouses like the first one they had built at the new Brydges Centre became a great outreach project for visiting mission teams, and several were built at various children's homes to help those homes become self-sufficient. Dave's gardener and friend John, who by now had become Dave's property manager and "right hand," was particularly interested in this aspect of the ministry and helped oversee these projects. Eventually the greenhouse-building led Dave to seek training on a new agricultural project in Africa called Farming God's Way. Dave and John learned this nutrient- and water-saving method of growing produce and began teaching it to Kenyan farmers.

Water projects continued to be another spoke of MpM's ministry. Through generous donations of supporters back home, the Bells were able to provide Chlorine Producing Units (CPUs) to several children's homes, allowing them to purify the tap water before using.

They also began working with the Maasai village of Inkiito to help them drill a borehole for the village of 600 people in a drought-ravaged section of Kenya. With the permanent water table 700 feet below the surface, the cost of drilling a well had scared away most potential assistance. But Dave met with the village and church elders, getting a commitment from them to share the burden, and some generous donors from the States made it possible for the villagers to enjoy fresh "sweet" water for the first time in their lives.

Yet another spoke of the ministry was the medical clinics with which Dave and Jen and visiting teams assisted. Working alongside Robyn Moore and other health professionals, clinics were conducted in various

children's homes, villages, and schools. Conducting medical clinics often led to opportunities for building greenhouses and most importantly sharing the gospel with the children and staff. Robyn's long-time ministry added many connections to the Bells' network and provided a variety of experiences and new venues for visiting mission teams to teach and witness. Often those medical clinics would uncover potentially fatal health conditions for orphans and the Bells worked to help get these children the medical intervention and treatment they needed.

Through all this ever-changing outside activity, one thing remained constant...babies continued to steadily stream through the MpM doors. By the time 2012 came to a close, the big house in Kitengela was beginning to feel tight with the Bell family of four plus the eleven rescued infants as well as the babies' caregivers. And so they began praying about their next move, a new property to house the growing infant rescue ministry and the financial means to secure it. A whole new God-sized challenge lay before them.

Mahali pa Maisha Infant Rescue Center   *Kitengela, Kenya*

CHAPTER 20

A Place to Call Home

August 2012

Rural area outside of Kitengela, Kenya

"Pole pole" (pronounced "po-lay po-lay.") The chant echoed back through the trekkers as they put one foot in front of the other. "Slowly, slowly."

The thirteen were exhausted, but still they methodically kept the steady rhythm going one pace at a time, some steps agonizingly taking two entire seconds to complete so that it often seemed as if the hikers were moving in slow motion or not at all. Just when they thought another step was impossible someone would shout out "Abby" or "Jacob" or "Ezra" and somehow just hearing those names gave the group a brief burst of energy to continue creeping upward.

Uhuru Peak, the summit of Africa's tallest peak Mt. Kilimanjaro in Tanzania, loomed before them. Dave and the other trekkers could see their finish line in sight, now if only they could finish strong. And slowly. Had it been just 5 ½ days ago that they'd taken the first step on this ambitious adventure? Now the peak was in reach, 19,341 feet above sea level. The excitement was palpable in the thin, oxygen-deprived air. On August 5, 2012, this committed group of Christian men and women successfully summited Uhuru Peak, making it to the roof of Africa.

For some it had been a chance to strengthen family connections, for some a desire to escape the world of cell phones and daily grind, for some a chance to mark Kili off their bucket lists, for some an opportunity to challenge themselves to do something seemingly impossible. But for all, the common reason why they had spent the past week of their lives climbing, (and many more weeks training in preparation), was to raise awareness and funds for their common passion: Mahali pa Maisha.

The babies were their ultimate inspiration. With a goal of raising $50,000 for the ministry, each trekker had solicited donation pledges. But more important than the money were the prayers. Each climber had chosen one little one from the infant rescue center – Abby or Jacob or Ezra or Nathan or Luke or one of several other babies back at MpM that knew nothing of climbing Mt. Kilimanjaro but in their few months of life had already climbed physical and emotional mountains much more challenging than Uhuru Peak.

The Kitengela home that had seemed so spacious a few years ago was now crowded. If Mahali pa Maisha was to continue growing, they needed a bigger facility. For the past couple of years, Dave and Jen had been praying about the situation, seeking God's guidance on where to make a permanent home for the infant rescue center. Quality property in the right location was difficult to find, and then actually purchasing land was very, very difficult for non-Kenyans. Earlier in 2012 Dave had found a ten-acre property that looked promising, even making a down-payment on it. But that had fallen through, a huge disappointment that caused Dave and Jen to wonder whether they were hearing God properly. Dave had sat down on a hill in the middle of the property and gazed all around him, picturing in his mind where he'd build the infant rescue center, where he'd site his home, where the best garden and greenhouse spots would be. He thought it would be perfect.

God thought otherwise and made it very clear this was not what He had chosen, closing the door to purchasing that property with a resounding slam. Back to square one.

Months later another possibility became available. The Salvation Army owned a rural property that hadn't been used for many years with several buildings and homes on the acreage that had been overgrown in vegetation. Lots of work and dollars would be needed, but the property had some real potential and once more Dave and Jen began dreaming.

Those dreams were quickly shattered as well. As the Salvation Army leadership changed just as the Bells began serious consideration of the property, so did the attitude and willingness to lease. Not only were the owners getting cold feet, Dave and Jen also discovered that the "empty" buildings were not really empty at all, that squatters had moved in and were living there. In Kenya, they learned, it is very difficult to displace squatters as the culture values possession over actual ownership. If they could even convince the Salvation Army leadership to lease them the property, a long and difficult and probably futile legal battle awaited to evict the trespassers. Coming to terms with the reality of the situation, the Bells had to once more shake their heads and dejectedly walk away. Another door slammed.

Trusting that despite the hurdles ahead of them a property would eventually be found, steadily the funding for that as-yet-unknown property continued to be donated. The vision was cast and Dave and Jen's faithful stateside supporters believed in the vision and the Bells' ability to make it happen. With a lofty goal of raising $350,000, they sometimes doubted whether they had set themselves up for failure. But slowly and steadily the fund grew as the Bells continued to seek God's will for the future home of Mahali pa Maisha.

Meanwhile the volume of babies and staff made it very difficult for the Bell family with their own two little ones, Ethan and Selah, to continually be under the same roof as all the infants. In mid-2013, another home right across the street in their Kitengela neighborhood opened up for rental, and the Bell family of four moved into that house, giving everyone a little much-needed breathing room. The new home, now the official headquarters of CSI in Kenya, was a quick 30-second walk from the other rental home which housed the babies, and it was a good temporary fix. But it was not a long-term solution.

Prayers and more prayers. Phone calls to real estate agents. Visits to potential sites that in reality had little potential at all for MpM's needs. More prayers. Antennae in the form of John and his brother Francis put out into the community for any possible available properties. Frustrations. Wondering what God's will really was. More prayers. And the babies kept coming.

Meanwhile, the pressure was on for the Bells to find a new location for Mahali pa Maisha soon. Both owners of both homes they were currently living in and using for the rescue center had decided to put those properties on the real estate market. Dave and Jen knew that if either one or both sold quickly, they'd find themselves in quite a bind. The clock was ticking.

Ever since moving to Kitengela, the Bells had driven by a well-developed property with a nice house that was owned by a prominent politician, Mzee George Saitoti. The Bells had met Mr. Saitoti a few times and knew him to be passionate about children's issues, so when a suspicious helicopter crash took his life in 2012, Dave and Jen wondered if perhaps his property might soon be up for sale. After Saitoti's death, the Bells intentionally drove past the property quite often in hopes that it might be on the market. One day in 2014 as they slowly cruised by, Dave and Jen felt God was insistently nudging them to inquire about it, but they had no idea who to contact. Dave mentioned his dilemma to John, who with a puzzled look responded that the pastor who had just officiated at his father-in-law's funeral was an advisor to the Saitoti family. Connection made! God's hands were all over this situation from the start.

As it turned out, that particular property was unavailable as it was still tied up in government red tape. But Mr. Saitoti's sister-in-law had some adjacent land and Dave and Jen drove out to see it.

As always, God's timing and provision proved to be perfect. Driving down the long, dirt lane lined with pink-bloomed bougainvilleas leading into the seven-acre property, a feeling of peaceful excitement filled both Dave and Jen. This was it, the place God intended for MpM's new home! Off a main highway yet easily accessible, the property was less than ten miles from their current Kitengela homes, which would allow the Bells to continue working alongside the same officials with whom they'd built trusting relationships. A twelve-foot-high established hedge would provide privacy and security, and there was already electricity running to the property.

A dream just waiting to come true! The wheels of Dave's brain were already turning, planning where they might build the rescue center as well as staff and private family housing and laying out possible garden plot and greenhouse locations in his mind's eye. There was plenty of room to create a spacious compound, yet not so much that it would have been impossible to adequately maintain.

Besides electricity, the other big necessity and always an unknown when building in Kenya was a generous water supply. Dave felt himself nearly holding his breath as hydrological surveys were conducted, and then exhaling a huge sigh of relief when all indications were that there was water under the property. Boreholes on surrounding properties were producing 5000-6000 liters per hour, a decent supply, but they were told by the Kenyan experts that they should expect to drill to 350 feet to get anywhere near that amount of water. An expensive proposition, to say the least, with no guarantees.

Without a dependable water supply there could be no infant rescue center.

"Where God guides, He provides." Dave looked up at the small sign on their living room shelf, given to them many years ago by a dear friend. How many hundreds of times had he needed that reminder? And how many hundreds of times had He provided, just as promised? But as much as Dave and Jen knew, indeed had LIVED that truth, there were still times of doubting and fretting. What if the water wasn't there? What if enough money didn't come in to build? What if…what if…what if….? God was sufficient, and many restless nights the Bells called upon that promise. Where God guides, He provides.

And provide He did! Knowing that Kenyan science was nowhere near American technology in such matters, before committing to the tremendous expense of drilling the borehole Dave hired his friend Mark Purington to repeat the hydrology tests using the new equipment he'd brought over from the States. Mark suggested the drilling be done 50 yards away from the Kenyan calculated location, his tests indicating that the original spot picked would not yield water. Trusting his friend's judgment and US technology over Kenyan educated guesswork, Dave told the drillers to use Mark's suggested location.

When the water permit was secured and it was time to drill the borehole, Dave and Jen hoped and prayed that there would be enough water pressure to adequately provide for not only the infant rescue center itself, but also for the other homes and buildings that would eventually dot the property. In November 2014 God answered their fervent prayer for water in an incredible way. Not only did water flow freely and bountifully from the new well, but it gushed out at the astounding rate of 14,000 liters per hour! Once more, God had exceeded their wildest expectations.

What a fitting metaphor for the free, precious, and abundant living water that the Bells so desperately wanted to spread to everyone around them. Water was a necessity of life, both physical life and spiritual life. God had richly blessed them with both…bountiful water for their bodies and more importantly an endless supply of living water for their souls through faith in their Savior Jesus.

Work on the property began. Scrub trees and brush were cleared away, a security fence and gate constructed, lots of different varieties of trees planted, drainage pipes installed, garden plots prepared, and greenhouses erected. One by one the buildings started going up, first the water tower and then foundations for the infant rescue center, team housing, staff housing, and finally the director's home.

But during all the turmoil surrounding the property, another turmoil was gradually coming to a head. Over the past year, the Bells had many times questioned their continued involvement with CSI. Their ministry had grown tremendously and was really outside the normal confines of the vision of Christian Service International, whose focus was on sending short-term teams to many locations across the globe. The transition to come under the CSI umbrella had been a good move at the time it happened as it allowed the freedom to develop the ministry as the Bells felt God was leading them. But with the main focus of CSI being on sending teams and the main focus of the MpM ministry to address specific challenges on the ground within Kenya, it became clear it was time to grow into an independent ministry with a single focus. With that in mind, Dave and Jen began the process of separating from CSI and setting up their own 501c3 non-profit in the US.

Dave and Jen solicited several faithful Christian supporters and formed a Board of Directors, legally incorporated Mahali pa Maisha, set up a small US office, and after hours of filling out the lengthy and complicated paperwork filed for nonprofit status in March 2015. In June of that year, the long-awaited and much-anticipated letter arrived from the IRS: Mahala pa Maisha Inc. was officially a 501c3 non-profit entity.

Meanwhile, back in Kenya, property projects consumed the bulk of Dave's time and energy, and there were certainly as many frustrating moments as joyous ones that year. Construction of facilities such as these would be a huge undertaking in the States, but exponentially more so in Kenya. The hassle of securing permits, hiring trustworthy contractors, finding reliable workers, and locating decent building materials were only the tip of the iceberg. Kenyan building techniques and standards were not even close to the American standards to which Dave was accustomed, and more than once Dave had to tear out and redo completed work that didn't meet his expectations. Costs of windows and doors fluctuated wildly, largely depending on who Dave talked to and their mood at the moment, and Dave often found himself at the mercy of the only supply source in town.

MpM Team Housing   2016

Many times over the course of what became a nearly-three-year building project, Dave and Jen felt like they were taking two steps forward only to have to take one or two (or sometimes even three) backward. But slowly, very slowly it seemed, one by one buildings were completed. In May of 2016 the team housing was finished and the Bells moved onto the property, temporarily sharing the team building with visiting teams while their home was being built. Shortly afterward, John and his family moved into the new manager's home, and in September 2016 the infant

MpM Infant Rescue Center   2016

rescue center was completed and all the infants and remainder of the staff moved to the property.

What a joy to have the entire Mahali pa Maisha family together! The director's home was the last to be completed, and in March 2017 Dave, Jen, Ethan, and Selah moved into the brand new director's home just inside the gated entrance of the Mahali pa Maisha campus. Only God knows what He has in store for this family whose hearts are sold out to His service, but until He tells them to "Go," this is where the Bells are content to lay their heads at night. Until He moves them or carries them into eternity with Him, a place to call Home.

MpM Director's House   2016

Epilogue

March 2017

Outside Kitengela, Kenya

The hot mid-day sun beat down on Dave's head as he reached the last step of the ladder. Beads of sweat trickled into his collar, the gentle breezes up so high in the air bringing welcome cooling relief from the heat and exertion. Catching his breath, he climbed off the ladder and onto the roof and slowly turned around to survey his world.

Dave had made countless treks to the top of the Mahali pa Maisha compound water tower, but each trip took his breath away.

Not so much because of the physical challenge of climbing the tall ladder, although now at 57 years old it was becoming more so all the time. No, Dave's breathlessness was due mostly to the awe that filled him. It never got old, the awe of where he was and how God had brought him to this place, to this ministry, to this season of his life.

Up here it was peaceful, the sounds of life on the property below muted by the distance. No matter how many times he surveyed the complex of Mahali pa Maisha, Dave was still amazed at God's provision of this beautiful property and the funds to build the needed facilities. From here he could see the entire seven acres dotted with houses filled with life...the manager's home where John lived with his wife and two children, the director's home for the four Bells, the team building which housed visitors, and the largest and most important structure on the grounds, the infant rescue center. Dave smiled as he watched his still-lovely bride Jen toting MpM's newest arrival across the yard toward their home. Oh how she adored those babies and oh how he adored her! When they'd said "I do" to each other 34 years ago, neither of them could have possibly imagined the roads down which God would lead them. What a journey it had been, and Dave prayed they would travel yet many more roads together. He could hear Ethan and Selah's carefree laughter as they bounced together on the trampoline so far below his feet. Two young children who weren't much older than his two grandsons back in Indiana, many times Dave had wondered if perhaps he and Jen were crazy taking on such responsibility in mid-life. But what joy and energy they brought and Dave and Jen couldn't imagine life without them. Across the way his trusted right-hand manager and one of his best friends in the world, John patiently and methodically worked his way down the garden rows. What a God-send John had proved to be!

Although Dave couldn't see them from where he stood, the colorful lilac-breasted roller birds were singing, fussing really, nearby. The wind rustled the leaves of the acacia trees, and looking out beyond the property fence a trio of zebras contentedly grazed blissfully unaware of his presence. Up here he was alone with his thoughts...alone except for the mighty presence of his mighty God.

As Dave's eyes surveyed this small corner of the world that God had entrusted, for a time, to Jen and him, his thoughts traveled 8000 miles to the other side of the world where the rest of his precious family lived. Chris and Ariel now had two beautiful sons, Miles and Paxton,

Dave and Jen's grandchildren that most of the year they adored from afar. Nate was busy living his life, fulfilling his dream to be a chef. Dave's parents Myron and Phyllis were aging too, and Jen's father Earl was also feeling the effects of many years on this earth. And they missed their siblings, their nieces and nephews, their close friends back in the States. It was by far the hardest part of being a missionary, being away from family and friends. But no matter how much they adored those so far away, obedience to God was always their top priority and Dave and Jen prayed that their example of service would impact their loved ones back home.

Eyes filled with tears of gratitude, Dave once more thanked his Heavenly Father for the innumerable yet undeserved blessings that God had showered upon him. Grace that was sufficient to cover all of his many shortcomings, Dave could never praise God enough for choosing him to do His work.

And smiling through his tears, he silently thanked his earthly father Myron for the best advice he'd ever received, a lesson that Dave needed as a young child trying to keep up with a melting ice cream cone and a lesson he had needed and used nearly every day since.

Don't miss out on a single drop of the sweet goodness.

"Lick and turn."

Forever in Their Hearts

July 2017

To date, 141 abandoned infants have found a place of life at Mahali pa Maisha.

While it is necessary for the Bells to track such things, 141 is not just a statistic. Each one of those 141 precious, innocent children of God was unique, with his/her own background story, with his/her own personality and gifts, with his/her own future and purpose in God's kingdom.

When the Bells receive a call to pick up a new baby, that child is brought to live in the Bells' family home for a week or more. Jen, (or Ma Bell, as Dave affectionately calls her), carefully bathes, weighs, examines, and documents each new life entrusted to their care. Most come unnamed, and God places a name on her heart for each child, which may be changed by the adoptive parents when the child is legally adopted into his or her forever family.

The new arrival lives under Ma Bell's devoted care as she screens them for potential health issues, analyzes their individual needs, and gets them on a regular schedule. When they are deemed healthy and ready, the baby is transferred to the infant care center and placed under the care of the staff there. Rarely is the Bell home without a new baby, and many times there are several staying with them at the same time. The Bells will certainly never forget the time there were five infants under the age of three weeks living under their roof! A full, uninterrupted night of rest is a rarity for Jen and Dave, but the rewards of seeing those tiny babes thrive is worth every sleepless moment.

Rescued babies live at the MpM infant center while they grow and until an adoptive family is matched with them. Kenyan law does not permit adoption until at least six months of age unless the birth mother willingly signs paperwork releasing her newborn for adoption, circumstances the Bells rarely encounter as most babies are abandoned or taken out of parents' custody by officials. Mahali pa Maisha is registered to care for up to thirty children with a target age of zero to two years of age. The Bells have never turned a baby away, and oftentimes their numbers swell, at one point to as high as 33 infants, until the courts can get adoption papers in order for the older babies. Well over half of the infants from MpM are adopted into new families, with the remainder usually being placed back into the care of their parents or another family member, often despite the futile protests of Dave. Many tears of frustration have been shed by the Bells over the years as they've been forced to follow court mandates and put babies back into the hands of families ill-equipped to provide for their needs. But for at least a few months of their short lives, these little ones have felt the love and compassion of Jesus.

Jen can remember each one of those 141 babies and most of the circumstances and details surrounding their stay at MpM. Every single one of those little human "starfish" is precious to both her and Dave and will never be forgotten. But there are a few children that stand out, who in their brief stays carved out an extra-special place in the Bells' hearts.

Jamal John (JJ) came under Dave and Jen's care in March 2011, before Mahali pa Maisha was officially registered. JJ was living at a children's home, estimated to be about twelve months old and barely weighing over twelve pounds. At Nurse Robyn's insistence, the severely malnourished boy with the tale-tell grotesquely distended belly was taken in by the Bells and loved on in their home for just a little over a month.

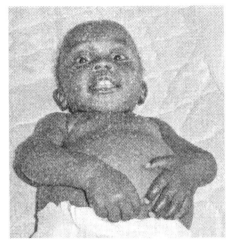

JJ   March 2011

Michael Moses was also living with them at that time, and Michael and JJ immediately became best friends, doing everything together, and the two of them were Dave's special buddies. Dave would greet little JJ by putting his fist out to him and saying, "Hook me up!" JJ would respond by giving him a fist bump back with a huge toothy grin.

Michael & JJ   March 2011

Fearing JJ would never survive under the care of the home where he'd previously been, the Bells worked with the District Children's Officer and, despite threats from that home's director, when JJ was healthy enough he was transferred to the much more reputable children's home where Michael had also been sent. The Bells hoped, as in Michael's case, to move him to the home for his safety and protection then to pursue adopting him.

In mid-September that same year, Dave and Jen were at the Nairobi airport getting ready to fly back to the States for their annual furlough when Dave's phone rang. It was the director of the children's home, informing them that JJ was gravely ill and had been taken to the hospital. Just as they were boarding the plane, she called again with the devastating news that JJ had passed away. Later they would find out that the cause of death was an undetected enlarged heart.

JJ, despite his short life, left a legacy of joy to all who knew him. And Dave and Jen would forever remember with a smile his big goofy grin that would light up the darkest of moods.

Abigail Susan (Abby) was the first admittance after Mahali pa Maisha had been legally registered as a CCI (Charitable Children's

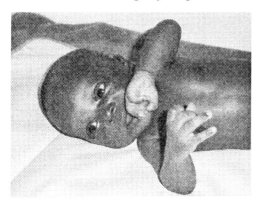

Institution), coming into the Bells' lives on January 30, 2012. Abby had been living at a less-than-desirable children's home, of which Kenya has way too many. That January day Dave got a call from the children's officer asking them to make an emergency rescue, that even though the home had been ordered by the

Abby January 2012

government to no longer take in infants, it continued to do so.

Upon arrival at MpM, Abby was severely malnourished and suffering from neglect. Rashes covered her little body, a result of not being cleaned. Under Jen's care, Abby responded very quickly to proper nutrition, care, and prayer, and grew into a happy toddler. Abby was MpM's first adoption in September 2012.

Sarah Elizabeth was born prematurely on a rainy night in late November 2012, a tiny bundle left in a cold driving rain outside the gate of a children's home near Kitengela. When the home, which was not staffed or equipped to care for infants, discovered her the next morning, they took her to a small nearby hospital and called the police. The police, in turn, called Dave and the Bells went to the hospital to pick up the newborn.

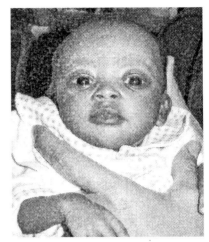

Sarah   December 2012

She was the tiniest baby either of them had ever held, obviously premature and weighing just over 2.5 pounds. Even more critical than her diminutive size was her dangerously low body temperature of 95.5 degrees Fahrenheit.

Having no better means to warm her up, the Bells wrapped her in the expensive down jacket Dave had purchased and used when he climbed Kilimanjaro just a few months before. Placing hand warmers in the pockets, they wrapped the tiny child inside and tucked the bundle into bed with a hot water bottle. Often Dave or Jen would lie in bed with Sarah next to their skin to help warm up her little body.

After ten long days of slow progress, finally her body temperature reached normal and stabilized. Still extremely tiny and fragile, Sarah had already beaten the odds just by making it ten days. Then when Robyn examined her at two weeks of age, she discovered Sarah had another hurdle to face. A heart murmur. And then again at four weeks, when the Bells took Sarah for routine bloodwork the results showed her to be HIV+.

So many prayers across the globe went up for this tiny child of God. Sarah definitely had huge mountains to scale herself…this tiny infant who spent the first ten days of her life wrapped in a mountain-climbing jacket had health issues bigger than Kilimanjaro. And yet, proving He loves even the smallest of his children, God answered prayers. A second more definitive HIV test called a PCR came back negative. Apparently the initial test results were a result of Sarah's birth mother being HIV+ and those antibodies showing up in Sarah's newborn body. Thankfully God's healing and Jen's prescribed healthy diet prevented Sarah from contracting the AIDS virus herself.

By mid-February 2013, Sarah's heart murmur was still noticeable so Robyn referred her to Tenwek Hospital, a mission hospital in western Kenya run by World Gospel Mission. As the expert cardiologist listened to Sarah's heart, he didn't detect any abnormality and declared that the murmur had "mysteriously" gone away. Once more, God had healed little Sarah!

Having triumphantly scaled her mountains, Sarah started gaining weight and rapidly caught up with her developmental milestones. At the age of nine months and weighing an amazing 15.5 pounds, Sarah was adopted into her very own forever family. She was truly a miraculous display of the power of the Great Physician.

Ave Maria was one of four babies Dave and Jen brought home one day in April 2014. The children's officer met Dave and Jen at a private hospital that wasn't supposed to have abandoned infants yet had several little ones, none of them getting the attention they needed. The children were kept in the beds unless visitors came, at which time they paraded the babies around in an effort to raise funds for the hospital.

When the Bells brought Ave to Mahali pa Maisha, she was 22 months old and weighed 18 pounds. In the nearly two years of her life, Ave had rarely been out of her crib and the only attention she got all day was when someone fed her a bottle.

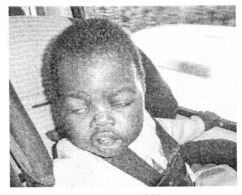

Ave   April 2014

Strapped into her into the van car seat to take her to MpM, Ave seemed almost comatose, staring out the window chewing her tongue and cheek until they were raw. Her teeth were discolored due to a lack of calcium and her body had a foul odor because she was rarely bathed. Lesions covered her private areas. In short, Ave was a physical and emotional mess.

For the first two weeks at MpM, Dave and Jen believed Ave to be deaf and mute, as she had absolutely no reaction to the loud banging of pans just behind her. She made no effort to sit up and had little muscle tone. Then one day after Ave had been there about a month, Jen heard sounds coming from Ave's room. She, along with a couple of other toddlers who shared that same room, was supposed to be napping. Jen quietly opened the door only to find Ave softly singing a song the caregivers sing to the MpM babies, "Baby Jesus, Baby Jesus, I love you...."

Clearly Ave was not deaf or mute at all! Jen was astonished that she could hear and talk. A visit to an audiologist for an extensive hearing test revealed Ave's hearing was nearly perfect. She had simply shut down from the lack of human interaction during her first 22 months of life.

With lots of tender loving care and lavished with attention, Ave soon became a whole new little girl. She began saying words and crawling, which soon progressed to walking and running. She gained weight and was soon talking like a normal two-year-old. Like night becomes day, she went from a withdrawn emotional wreck to a very happy and bright little girl.

When a Swedish couple adopted Ave in March 2015, one would never have imagined her to be the same little baby who had been in a near vegetative state just one year earlier. Ave is now thriving and loving life with her new family.

Jesse David came into the Bells' lives and hearts in June 2015. An innocent product of a highly-taboo incestual relationship between cousins, one-month-old Jesse was being sought after by the villagers who were wanting to kill him. Babies like Jesse were considered curses and in their tribal culture had to be killed.

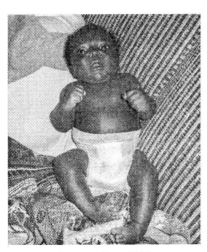

Jesse   June 2015

Immediately it was clear that Jesse was a special little guy. Dave had a long drive home in heavy traffic, giving him a chance to talk and sing to Jesse and to pray for this precious little boy and for a culture that could consider any newborn child a curse.

For the most part Jesse was healthy. Except his feet, both of which were severely clubbed, with the bottoms of his feet naturally facing each other squarely. Sores were on his ankles and feet, indicating that someone had unsuccessfully tried to correct his malformation by a primitive method.

When the Bells had a doctor examine Jesse, their fears were confirmed. His feet would require some very extensive work. The occupational therapist assigned to Jesse's case estimated it would take at least twenty different castings, each one forcing his feet a little more back into a normal position, followed by a minimum of three surgeries to correct the clubbing. Then, perhaps, Jesse might be able to hobble around but certainly he would never run like a normal child.

The castings began in October and they were brutal, excruciatingly painful for Jesse and causing tears of empathy to flow for Dave and Jen as they held Jesse down. Thankfully the therapist understood the burden to travel into Nairobi each week for the castings, so he graciously came to MpM and worked on Jesse there. Each time Jesse's ankles were forced to twist past their range of motion. Despite the pain, Jesse was a trooper. While he would whimper during the castings, he was all smiles most of the time and eventually began dragging the heavy casts, which ran from his hips to his toes, around on the floor with him.

By mid-January 2016 the castings were finished, and everyone involved was astonished at the miraculous healing God had given Jesse. No surgery would be needed. Jesse would continue to wear a brace for 22 hours of each day, holding his feet at the proper angle to allow his leg bones to grow strong in a near normal position. Each day the MpM caretakers did therapy with Jesse to help build his leg muscles.

By the middle of February Jesse was crawling and attempting to stand. By the time he was 13

months old, his braces were only worn at night and the little boy that doctors said would never walk defied all odds and did just that!

When Jesse went home with his forever family in September 2016, not a few tears of joy were shed as the Bells and the caretakes said good-bye. Jesse's new older brother now had a soccer buddy since by that time Jesse was running around like any normal 16-month-old toddler. Another true miracle!

No doubt there will be other special babies whose cries and giggles will grace the rooms of MpM in future days, children abandoned and unloved by society whose only hope for life is a miracle. But the Bells have witnessed God's incredible power over and over and over again, the worse the circumstances, the greater the life-giving miracle. That's their passion, their purpose, what Mahali pa Maisha is all about. It truly lives up to its name. A place for life!

On a Personal Note

"Go, send, or disobey." --John Piper

I've known David Bell all my life. Or I guess I should say all of his life, since I'm three years older. We grew up as part of the same little country congregation at White Branch Church of the Brethren, where his family (the Bells/Bowmans) and my family (the Houses/Stockbergers) each filled the pews on their own side of the sanctuary. David's sister Jeanna was one of my very best friends growing up, and my sisters and I and the Bell clan all rode on the same school bus driven by the late Howard Tucker.

After I left home, I lost touch with many of my childhood friends, including the Bells. I got married and busy with my own family, occasionally running into someone from the Bell family at White Branch events or in our small Hagerstown, Indiana community. It wasn't until I began attending Bible Study Fellowship myself that our paths seriously crossed again.

The house Dave and Jen bought on Indiana Highway 38 and where they built and established Cutting Edge was just around the corner from my County Line childhood home. Like other neighbors, Dad wasn't any too thrilled about the start of that business in his territory, but he soon came around. For reasons only God knew at the time, He continued criss-crossing my life with the Bells over the years.

When I heard that Dave and Jen had sold their home and business to move to Africa, I was one of the naysayers. My husband Kim and I had always supported missionaries, but I was shocked at their willingness to uproot their children and leave their families to move halfway across the world. I just didn't understand.

Now I do. As we began supporting the Bells both prayerfully and financially, we found ourselves becoming more and more invested in their ministry. Kim and I got our Sulphur Springs Christian Church family involved too, and we've made two amazing visits to Kenya, witnessing first-hand the life-saving ministry of MpM. We are also blessed to serve on the US Board of Directors for Mahali pa Maisha, and we count Dave and Jen among our dearest friends.

Jesus's last words to his followers as he ascended into Heaven are written in Matthew 28: 19-20. *"Go therefore and make disciples of all nations, baptizing them in the name of the Father and of the Son and of the Holy Spirit, teaching them to observe all that I have commanded you. And behold, I am with you always, to the end of the age."*

It was not a suggestion, it was a command. Every believer has an obligation to do his/her part to spread the gospel to the ends of the earth. Most of us will not be called to leave our homes and move to the other side of the world to teach the gospel, but we are ALL called to do our part in sharing the good news of the saving grace of Jesus.

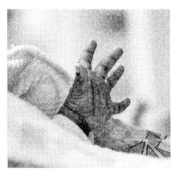

The Bells are "go-ers." Kim and I are "senders." Every obedient believer must be either one or the other.

Terry Gray, July 2017

For more information about

Mahali pa Maisha:

Website:

www.mpmkenya.org

Emails:

dbell@mpmkenya.org

jbell@mpmkenya.org

usoffice@mpmkenya.org

Kenya Field Address:
(personal correspondence)
Dave and Jen Bell
PO Box 128-00242
Kitengela, Kenya   East Africa

US Office (donations):
Mahali pa Maisha
PO Box 262
Sulphur Springs, IN 47388

About the Author

Terry Gray was born and reared in rural Indiana, enjoying an idyllic childhood growing up on the County Line Road with her parents and three younger siblings. Following graduation from Hagerstown High School, Terry pursued her education at Indiana University, earning a Master of Science degree in Elementary Education.

She began dating her husband, Kim, after she started teaching and coaching at the same country school that they both had attended. Little did they know, but their marriage had been "arranged" by their fathers years before; in August 2017 they will celebrate 37 years of marriage.

Kim and Terry make their home in a country cabin on 35 acres in central Indiana, rearing four wonderful children who have flown the nest and have families of their own. They love country life, and unashamedly dote on their eight young, beautiful grandchildren.

Terry works part-time as the office administrator for their church, volunteers as the US office administrator for Mahali pa Maisha, tries to stay fit by working out and playing tennis when she can. She and her husband Kim serve on the US Board of Directors for MpM. Her passions are her faith and family, along with lots of hobbies including photography, beekeeping, traveling, and blogging (www.notquitecountrygirl.com). In 2015, Terry authored her first memoir entitled *Unsinkable*. This is her second book.

And, not one to be left out concerning ice cream or life, Terry also is known to regularly do her own licking and turning!